BIRDS OF SINGAPORE

AND

SOUTH-EAST ASIA

BIRDS OF SINGAPORE
AND SOUTH-EAST ASIA

SIR JOHN A.S. BUCKNILL

AND

F.N. CHASEN

With thirty-one coloured plates by G.A. Levett-Yeats

GRAHAM BRASH, SINGAPORE

© This edition, Graham Brash (Pte) Ltd, 1990

First published in 1927
This edition first published in 1990 by
Graham Brash (Pte) Ltd
227 Rangoon Road
Singapore 0821

ISBN 9971-49-178-8

Cover by Matthew Lau
Printed in Singapore by
Loi Printing Pte Ltd

PUBLISHER'S NOTE

First published in 1927, this book was originally entitled *The Birds of Singapore Island*. But, as pointed out in the Introduction and will be seen in their "Distribution", the birds described in the book are to be found not only in Singapore but throughout South-east Asia. For this reason, it is felt that *Birds of Singapore and South-east Asia* would be a more accurate title. It is to be borne in mind, however, that there are many birds in the region which are not found in urbanised Singapore and therefore not included in this book. Nevertheless, this revived classic will serve as a very helpful guide to the more common birds in South-east Asia, even South China and the Indian sub-continent.

PREFACE

DURING his tenure of the Directorship of the Raffles Museum, Singapore, my predecessor there, the late Major J.C. MOULTON, O.B.E., M.A., D.SC., projected in collaboration with SIR JOHN A.S. BUCKNILL, then Chief Justice of the Straits Settlements, a little book on Forty Common Birds of Singapore to be illustrated by coloured plates. The work was interrupted by Major MOULTON'S transfer to Sarawak as Chief Secretary to Government and, as his successor in the Raffles Museum, I fell heir to the illustrations, Sir JOHN BUCKNILL'S MS. and some notes of Major MOULTON'S which he hoped to find time to put in order and complete so that the book could be produced as originally planned. This, however, proved impossible and Major MOULTON withdrew: I was thus under the necessity of providing a successor to him, for I lacked both the ability and inclination to write a popular book on birds myself.

Mr. F.N. CHASEN, Curator of the Raffles Museum, agreed to undertake the task and we decided that the scope of the volume should be extended to include all the common birds of the island and others less common as well. Mr. CHASEN set to work with such enthusiasm that, in editing his MS., I have had, regretfully, to abridge it considerably in order to keep this book within certain limits of size. Sir JOHN BUCKNILL'S notes on species figured have been made use of though, owing to the change of plan, they bulk proportionately smaller than was originally the case; and his contributions have his initials attached. Mr. A.W. HAMILTON has helped by supplying Malay names for many of the birds dealt with.

This book is intended for the use of the uninitiated, both residents and visitors, who wish to know something of the birds they may see about them in Singapore Island, but it will also be useful to the same class of student in British Malaya generally. It is written not so much for the ornithologist who makes a business of seeking birds as for him who is content to meet them.

C. BODEN KLOSS,
Director of Museums,
Straits Settlements and
Federated Malay States.

SINGAPORE, 16*th September,* 1926.

CONTENTS

LIST OF PLATES

BIRDS OF SINGAPORE AND SOUTH-EAST ASIA

INTRODUCTION.

FIELD WORK.

IN this brief introduction to the study of birds we hope that the reader will not expect to find directions for collecting eggs or skinning birds and preserving their skins for these points we have purposely omitted. The days in which the amateur's miscellaneous collection of skins from odd parts of the world was of value have almost disappeared and nowadays one has to look at the map very hard in order to discover territory in which haphazard collecting methods are justified. With an occasional exception the collecting of vertebrate animals is best left to trained collectors who collect with the minimum expenditure of life. It would be especially lamentable to shoot birds in Singapore as the fauna of the island is so rapidly being destroyed that the student of birds can best occupy himself with field work in the form of observation, for in this branch of local ornithology there is a great opportunity for research work. In fact we know so little of the life history of even the very common Malayan birds that almost any series of carefully made (and repeatedly checked!) observations are of value. Several points on which information is needed occur as we write and perhaps mention of these will be indicative of work that would be most useful.

In the first place very little is known about the movements of migratory birds in Singapore. The majority of our land birds, for instance the bulbuls, babblers, sunbirds, woodpeckers, barbets and king-crows are resident although some of them are subject to a certain amount of local movement. This means that they are breeding birds and are in the country all the year round. On the other hand a large number of species are migratory, either spending the winter in this country, their breeding grounds being further to the north, or merely visiting us in the spring and autumn on their journeys to and fro. These comings and goings are by no means clearly understood, for not only do the movements take place mainly at night but the actual times and to some extent the seasons of the movements are confused by the loitering of non-breeding birds of the same species and a hundred and one other complicated events. In Europe and in a few other parts of the world the phenomena of migration have been intensively studied and in certain cases the movements of a species are almost as well known as if the route and attendant circumstances were marked on a map!

How desirable it would be if we could do this in Malaya, or even if we understood the fundamentals of the situation well enough to distinguish between the two main streams of birds that arrive on our shores, the one roughly speaking from the north-east and the other from the north-west. Careful notes as to dates of the first appearance in Singapore and at places along the coasts of the cattle-egret, the migratory bee-eater, the scattered flocks of young shrikes, the lively wagtails and the mysterious passing of the flocks of black and white cuckoo-falcons would all help. Some of the migratory birds seem to travel south by using the small islands in the Straits of Malacca as stepping stones, others follow the mountain range down the back of the Peninsula. The Anamba Islands in the South China Sea swarm with non-resident birds in the autumn and it is probable that although most of the migratory bands follow the coast lines some of them migrate in a straight line directly to the south of their breeding grounds.

Next to migration the best field of investigation, and certainly an easier one to work in, lies in the breeding habits of our common local birds. By avoiding an endless repetition of records concerning well-known facts such as the position of the nest, number, size and colour of the eggs, etc. in common birds (although be it noted that even here much remains to be done) and paying attention to other many neglected points particularly useful results would accrue.

[2]

Special attention could be given to the dates when the birds were seen paying attention to each other for the first time in the season. From how many dapper males does the dowdy little hen of the magpie-robin (a common bird in Singapore) select her mate? Not less than three we believe! And having been "suited" when does nest-building begin and how do the small partners divide the work—does the cock bird do his share or does he often clear out for an hour or two to attend to business further afield? When the eggs are laid and the birds are brooding how many times a day does the hen take a flit round to stretch her wings; and when the young are hatched how many times an hour are they fed? When the same youngsters are full grown and can fly how long are they allowed to remain in the vicinity before being chased away to find territory of their own? Most important too, how many days do the eggs take to hatch; and then what is the period between the hatching of the chick, the first sprouting of the feathers and its departure from the nest?

Scores of other points could be mentioned and no doubt many occur to the reader. For a few years past we have paid particular attention to the breeding habits of the common bulbul of the Singapore gardens but in spite of a large mass of notes taken over a period of three springs we are yet minus the key-note to the whole of our observations, for we have not yet found out the exact time between the hatching of the chick and the point at which our information begins. We suspect it to be more than twelve hours and less than two days, but that is only a guess. When the point is settled the tale can be linked up and we shall then understand the essential points of the growth of our bulbul from the time it is hatched, and thence at intervals of about twelve hours, until it actually leaves the nest of its own accord. At the moment the observations are all plus x hours!

Enough has been said to indicate the manner in which the bird lover can occupy his leisure hours with a view to useful results and there is no location in the whole of this island in which birds cannot be studied.

REFERENCE to a map is a very wise step as a preliminary to a study of any branch of natural history for the veriest beginner in such matters must realise that the character of the fauna of a country depends largely on its geographical position.

In our own corner of the world here in south-eastern Asia certain things are very difficult to explain. Elephants for instance are only found truly wild in the Malay Peninsula and Sumatra, likewise the tapir. Borneo and Sumatra share that great anthropoid ape the Orang utan; tigers are common to the Malay Peninsula, Sumatra and Java but are not found in Borneo and the nearest relatives of various common Javanese birds turn up in Indo-China and Burma! The birds of Great Britain and Japan, countries separated by the width of Europe and Asia are much more nearly allied than are those of Borneo and New Guinea, two islands only about eight hundred miles apart.

Attempts to divide the world into definite "zoological regions" or "realms" were made as early as the end of the eighteenth century, but it was not until 1857 that the late P. L. Sclater, at one time Secretary of the Zoological Society of London, outlined the six regions which are still accepted as more or less satisfactory by naturalists. Singapore is in the "Indian" or "Oriental" Region and Wallace notes that this small, compact but rich and varied area is characterised by the possession of many peculiar families and genera of land birds. Singapore belongs to the *Malaysian Sub-region of the Oriental Region.* This smaller division includes the Malay Peninsula, Sumatra, Borneo, Palawan, Java, Bali and many adjacent small islands. With the possible exception of Java, Bali and Palawan which seem to have been longest isolated within it we find that all over this sub-region the animals of the lowlands are very similar and there are no marked differences in the garden birds of any part of this area. The birds of the mountains show a strong relationship to those of the Himalayas.

The sub-region as outlined above can be broadly characterised by the presence of the orang-utan, the siamang, the flying-lemur and the beautiful argus-pheasant. The probable recent geographical changes in the "Malay Archipelago" are happily discussed by Wallace in several of his books and perusal of his accounts will show how by the submersion of one island and by the elevation of other land here and there the Malaysian fauna has been divided and re-united several times, thus accounting for some of the knotty points in the distribution of some species mentioned above. The effect of such changes are easier to appreciate when one realizes that a very moderate depression, Wallace says perhaps 500 feet, would convert Borneo into an island shaped something like Celebes; while if the sea-bottom were raised half that amount, the Peninsula, Sumatra, Java, Borneo and Bali would all become again parts of one great land-mass.

    *   *   *   *

As may be expected the birds of Singapore are very similar to those of Johore and the neighbouring countries. A year or two ago* we summarized the bird life and conditions of the island as follows : —

"The avifauna of Singapore Island is characteristic of the lowlands of the southern half of the Malay Peninsula. No striking anomalies are presented. The Waders, other migrants, and the few sea-fowl that approach the port are species just as frequently met with on the coasts of the Straits of Malacca.

"The present absence of any extent of old jungle is now responsible for the great scarcity, or even total absence, of certain species not uncommon in Johore, although it is easy to believe that some of these birds occurred on the island before the settlement was so large. The gradual extension of the city must perforce drive the birds away. It is stated that a few years ago green pigeons were to be seen in the Raffles Museum compound and kingfishers flew up and down the canal in Stamford Road. Such events are now remarkable. So far as birds are concerned, Singapore is not the home of the luxuriant, thriving life one is led to expect after digesting the literature dealing with natural history in the tropics.

---

*"*The Singapore Naturalist*", Vol. I., No. 2, April 1923.

"During the last two years the writer remembers whole days spent in the field with unprofitable results, including a week-end in the Bajau district at the end of the Chua Chu Kang Road with scarcely the sight of a bird, and other disastrous outings. But there are saving graces. Even on the return journey of the unsuccessful trip to Bajau, very late at night, a large fishing-owl flying low over the car for quite a long distance was a redeeming feature; and there are memories of delightful days spent in bird-watching chiefly in the western half of the Island, days when there were interesting birds to be seen at almost every turn of the river, blue bitterns flying from the mangrove before the approach of the sampan, large wary king-fishers splashing into the water in tern-like fashion yet further up stream and sun-birds of four or five species all seen in a morning. The sight of family parties of cuckoo-shrikes and baby pittas in the mangrove is satisfactory work for one day.

"The scarcity of even our resident birds is, without doubt, to a great extent due to the clearing of the island with the spread of the town but it is clear that the week-end 'sportsman' has wrought terrible havoc. A youth armed with a gun is a factor not to be ignored. Such a person shoots at everything he sees and I have seen such individuals returning from a shoot carrying a bunch of bulbuls strung together by the necks. One has to only to visit the Botanic Gardens in the late afternoon or early morning of any day to note the good results which it is possible to obtain by rigidly protecting birds, for there, more of the beautiful black and white songsters, *Copsychus musicus* (the Magpie Robin) can be seen in one hour than in most other districts on the island in a week.

"The writer is frequently asked as to the whereabouts of the best places for bird-watching on the island, but he would recommend that each person should find out the best places for himself for in the process we are likely to gain new observations.

"As a hint, however, we could mention that probably as many birds could be seen by an observer sitting on the top of Bukit Timah as in any other selected locality. Working the mangrove of the rivers and creeks is apt to be rather dull.

[6]

One works long for a little reward. Rubber estates are notoriously unproductive from a naturalist's point of view, and of jungle we have but a lamentably small area to deal with. Next to Bukit Timah we would suggest the rough country at the end of the Chua Chu Kang Road, then the Changi Jungle and above all the Botanic Gardens must not be forgotten.

"For a local bird-watching holiday Pulau Ubin is a good place because of its comparatively large area and close proximity to the mainland. The other outlying islands near Singapore are rather disappointing at most seasons of the year. About a dozen species are common to all the islands.

"The three common birds of Singapore Island are : —

1. The Tree Sparrow.
2. The Magpie Robin.
3. The Yellow-vented Bulbul.

"The first of these is to all intents and purposes the same species that is found in Europe.

"The tree-sparrow (*Passer montanus*) is found practically everywhere within the Singapore area. It has established itself on the lighthouses, it can be seen in the mangrove swamps and native kampongs and it hops about the roads and city gardens in the unconcerned manner displayed by its cousin, the house-sparrow (*P. domesticus*) in England.

"The magpie robin (*Copsychus musicus*) a dapper bird of about 'thrush-size' and piebald plumage (very like a miniature magpie) is also common, but unlike the sparrow does not consort in flocks. Its habits are more like those of the song-thrush at home. It has a most beautiful voice and fortunately can be seen in most parts of the island and the outlying districts. It nests in the gardens well within municipal limits.

"The yellow-vented bulbul (*Pycnonotus analis*) is also larger than the sparrow and is dingy in coloration. At a distance of a few yards it appears to be clad in sober brown plumage, lighter underneath, with a whitish head. Under the tail there is a patch of yellow. The bulbul is common enough in most localities. Like the Straits or magpie robin it breeds in the town gardens and its cheery gurgling note can be heard

[7]

by any resident as long as there is a patch of grass and a shrub or a few trees near the bungalow. The bulbul is one of the first birds in Singapore to get up in the morning and it is often abroad before even the sparrows have started to chatter."

In 1924 we paid especial attention to the small islands near Singapore and the following extract from our published paper may be worth quoting here* : —

"A map of Singapore and its environs shows that within a short distance, ranging from a matter of a few hundred yards from the coast, there are a number of smaller islands. Most of those with which the present paper is concerned can be readily seen from various points of the shore of Singapore.

"A few of these small islands are situated in the narrow strait running between Singapore and the mainland but the majority are to be found off the south coast, or as it would be more accurate to write, on account of the peculiar shape of Singapore Island—the south-west coast. Further afield, to the south again, one passes almost imperceptibly into that wonderful maze of islands known as the Rhio-Archipelago and politically Dutch.

"The sea between the most remote of the islands and Singapore only reaches 20 fathoms in a few places and is generally less than half that depth.

"It will be seen that the islands vary greatly in size. Pulau Ubin which is about 4½ x 1¼ miles and Pulau Tekong, approximately 4 x 2½ miles, being the largest; whilst others at high water show little else than the tops of mangroves. There seems to be no literature relating to these places although numerous papers have been published which deal in some detail with the fauna of the other islands situated in the Straits of Malacca and South China Sea off the western and eastern coasts of the Malay Peninsula.

"Ornithologically they are somewhat disappointing. Pulau Ubin and Pulau Tekong Besar have an avifauna which

---

*"*The Singapore Naturalist*", Vol. I., No. 3, May 1924, pp. 22—25.

probably rivals that of Singapore as regards number of species, and owing to their less populated state birds are by no means scarce. It is, however, somewhat misleading to include these two larger land masses with the smaller islands of the south coast, for their size and the varied nature of their topography attract birds of many families and most of the species found on them are, as in the case of Singapore, characteristic of the lowlands of the southern part of the Malay Peninsula.

"The smaller islands, on the other hand, certainly have a characteristic resident avifauna and in this point they present a uniformity which can only be matched by the monotony of their mangrove lined coastlines and similarity of general aspect.

"The list given at the end of the paper* contains the names of 106 species of birds which with the exception of *Penthoceryx sonnerati pravata* (Horsf.), *Arachnothera flavigaster* (Eyton) and *Trachycomus zeylandicus* (Gm.) are all known from Singapore. These three species will no doubt be recorded from the main island in the future but they are certainly by no means commonly met with.

"There is in fact, little, if anything, in the list, which is unexpected and this in itself is perhaps interesting.

"On the other hand there is a marked absence from the list of many common Malayan species, in a good number of cases these being birds which could be obtained with little difficulty a few miles away in the territory of Johore. Exhaustive collecting might fill in these omissions to some extent but there is no doubt that the avifauna of even Pulau Ubin and Pulau Tekong is largely influenced, firstly, by the separation from the mainland, narrow though the intervening strip of water is, and secondly by the absence of any extent of jungle. To the Timaliidæ in particular the last remark may be taken to apply.

"In the case of the smaller outlying islands the number of birds found is very small both in species and, usually, in individuals.

*Not printed here.

[9]

"A brief glance at the avifauna of the various other islands found off the coasts of the Peninsula will be helpful in enabling a slight comparison to be made with that of these nearer Singapore. Terutau Island, the Langkawi Islands and Pulau Jarak off the west coast and the Perhentians, Redangs and Tioman Island off the east coast as well as many others have all had their bird life investigated, although curiously enough Penang has been very neglected of late years. Many of these have their own special attractions.

"In the Langkawi group species either not known in the south of the Peninsula or only met with sporadically in that region are met with. Such are the wattled lapwing (*Sarcogrammus atronuchalis*), the big brown-winged kingfisher (*Rhamphalcyon amauroptera*) Swinhœ's bee-eater (*Melittophagus leschenaulti swinhœi*), the Burmese scaly-bellied woodpecker, (*Gecinus viridanus*) the Indian black-headed oriole (*Oriolus melanocephalus*) and the Burmese yellow-breasted sunbird (*Cyrtostomus flammaxillaries*), some of them at about southern limit of their range. Here also the beautiful stork, *Xenorhynchus asiaticus*, is found breeding. Hornbills of several species are common and in the lime-stone caves two species of the tiny *Collocalia* swifts breed. In the winter interesting fly-catchers and other land birds are met with as migrants.

"Mr. H. C. Robinson (Journal F.M.S. Mus. 1917, vol. vii, p. 129) says of Langkawi:—'It will be seen that the avifauna presents the same general characters as those of all the other groups of islands in the vicinity of the Malay Peninsula, namely, a great scarcity of all the more strictly jungle frequenting species belonging to the great family of Timaliidæ and the total absence of Eurylæmidæ, though we find a few species of Trogons, Barbets and Woodpeckers, orders which are entirely absent from the islands off the coast of Pahang on the east side of the Peninsula, these islands being smaller in extent and separated from the mainland by broader stretches of deeper water. Owing to the fact that our visit took place in the winter months, migratory flycatchers, thrushes and warblers are well represented while a considerable number of shore birds were also obtained or observed.'

"The Nicobar pigeon (*Calœnas nicobarica*) essentially a denizen of small islands, is now also known from a number of the islands near the Malayan coast. Pheasants and partridges are absent but the jungle-fowl has been recorded from Koh Samui off the Bight of Bandon, N. E. Coast, although Robinson in recording the fact suggested that they may have been introduced by the Siamese population of the island.

"The reef-heron (*Demiegretta sacra*) seems to be met with more or less commonly on most of the islands off the Malayan coast.

"From the Tioman group interesting marine birds have been recorded. Frigate birds occur and there are breeding colonies of two terns (*Sterna anœtheta* and *S. sumatrana*).

"From Pulau Jarak the booby (*Sula sula*) is reported.

"In the case of Pulau Ubin and P. Tekong it seems scarcely reasonably to compare them with the islands mentioned above and this chiefly on account of their close proximity to the mainland. They are very similar to Singapore in their avifauna.

"Large game-birds do not occur, babblers are very scarce —the jungle loving species absent. Likewise many other birds met with more or less commonly in the lowland jungles of the Peninsula are as yet unrepresented in the collections made on these islands. To mention but three, *Chloropsis icterocephala*, *Rubigula cyaniventris* and *Oriolus xanthonotus*. Hornbills, if they occur, only do so at intervals. The presence of three species of barbets, nine species of woodpeckers and two species of broadbills on Pulau Ubin is interesting.

"The reef-heron although it is found as near as Sultan Shoal seems too chary of coming close enough to Singapore to occur in the islands frequently. The frigate birds and the booby also keep well away to sea and there are no breeding colonies of terns. The Nicobar pigeon has not been obtained and probably comes no nearer than Pulau Pisang off the west coast of Johore.

"Leaving these two larger islands and turning to those to the south of Singapore we find a different state of affairs.

"Only a few species of birds are common here. Two or perhaps three species of sunbirds (*Anthreptes malaccensis, Cyrtostomus ornatus* and *Chalcostetha calcostetha*) are the most noticeable features of the bird-life and with the addition of the kingfishers (*Halcyon chloris humii, Rhamphalcyon capensis malaccensis* and *Alcedo b. bengalensis*), the inevitable magpie-robin (*Copsychus s. musicus*), a bulbul (*Pycnonotus p. plumosus*), a tree-starling (*Aplonis panayensis strigatus*), a tailor-bird (*Orthotomus r. ruficeps*), and two species of swallows (*Hirundo rustica gutturalis* and *H. j. javanica*), the list is almost exhausted. Other birds of course are found occasionally.

"The tiong (*Gracula j. javana*), and a woodpecker (*Dinopium j. javanense*) are frequently seen and perhaps should be added to the short list just given.

"Waders of course occur in season. The common sandpiper (*Tringoides hypoleucus*) is always the common species and is to be found in most months of the year. The turnstone (*Arenaria interpres*), is more numerous than is generally supposed and the whimbrel always outnumbers the curlew. Sandplovers of several species are likewise abundant. It is a significant fact that certain species of migratory birds which, in winter, occur on the mountains of the Malay Peninsula and on islands in the Straits of Malacca, are not included in the collections made and furthermore these species are as yet unrecorded from Singapore. Such are *Hemichelidon fuliginosa, H. ferruginea, Polyomyias mugimaki, Cichoselys sibiricus* and *Larvivora cyanea*. The last two also occur in the lowlands.

"The absence of any high mountains in the extreme south of the Peninsula may possibly have a bearing on this point."

ON THE NOMENCLATURE OF BIRDS

THE inclusion of a fair crop of technical names in the few preceding pages reminds us that it is now well nigh time that we attempted to elucidate the question of those much abused "Latin" terms which will be found plentifully scattered throughout this book.

First of all for a general justification for their use at all and then a few words about the manner in which they are formed and employed.

In the museum we are continually asked why things are not labelled with "readable and understandable" English names. Well, nowadays we endeavour to do this, rather against our inclination we might say, and the result is sometimes amusing!

It will be readily understood that many of the tiny creatures inhabiting this country have not yet had English names applied to them and in a good number of cases we have had to manufacture a name. The result has not always been pretty or euphonious. There seems little point in labelling a bird for instance as a "babbler"—one must say something else about it because a few hundreds of different kinds of babbler are already known. Many of these are very alike in size and plumage and one soon uses up the available geographical adjectives "Malayan babbler", "Sumatran babbler", etc., and also the descriptive "blue-faced", "brown-backed", "spotted", etc. A certain outlet is provided by the use of the name of the naturalist who first described the bird and so we can go on for a bit longer—Smith's babbler, Brown's babbler, Jones' babbler and so on but sooner or later the sticking point comes and then it is that one is forced to such names, (almost sentences) as the "Himalayan golden-backed three-toed woodpecker" or "the small eastern orange-breasted flycatcher" both of which have recently appeared in print, the first in a list of Indian birds and the later in a handlist of the birds of Borneo. It may be mentioned that a naturalist of *any nationality* would immediately recognise the first bird as *Tiga shorii* and the second as *Poliomyias luteola* but still the authors of these lists in deference to the public demand gave "English and understandable names" to all their birds. We were once rather amused at the dilemma of an ornithological friend of ours. He had just discovered a new species of bulbul from Siam and, I suppose, the description took him about five minutes to write out. But the editor of the journal to whom the description was to be sent always insisted on the inclusion of popular names in accepted papers and thus the difficulty began and three pipes later the two of us, for my assistance in this grave matter had been invoked, were no nearer to the finding of a suitable name for a Siamese bulbul. Bulbuls are so numerous in the East that all the more or less reasonable names were used up! The situation was met by inserting a not altogether proper name in the manuscript which as we anticipated the editor noticed and altered to his taste. We regret that the same plan of campaign is not likely to answer in this book and we have therefore done our best to provide suitable English names for all the birds mentioned, maintaining at the same that it is just as easy and far more convenient to call birds by technical names (although perhaps some of us pronounce them rather badly) as otherwise. In this application of names we have been as honest as possible and have not, like the curator of a small museum at home, who got over the difficulty (his committee of management said that he had got to provide "readable" names on the specimens) somewhat in this fashion—*Hemicercus sordidus* or the "Sordid Hemicercus", *Corydon sumatranus* or the Sumatran Corydon, *Cacomantis sepulchralis* or the Grave-like Cacomantis, etc.

The general idea underlying the binomial (or better, binominal) system of nomenclature is now generally understood and we will not insult our readers intelligence with a dissertation upon the system which was formally introduced by Linnæus of giving every species of animal a generic name and a specific name thus—*Corvus corax, Corvus corone, Corvus frugilegus, Corvus monedula*, these in order being the raven, the carrion crow, the rook and the jackdaw (here we may remark that popular names are quite useful when applied to very well-known birds in a broad sense).

The more recent developments in zoological nomenclature are not so well-known (where known in fact they are almost just as frequently misinterpreted) and as they are followed in this book, it is perhaps wise to explain their meaning. In most cases throughout the following pages it will be noticed that the technical name consists not of two but of three words. The abbreviated name at the end makes four but that is only the name of the person who described the species and is always printed in different type—not being part of the name. This trinomial system, which met with a very stormy reception on its introduction is now universally used (there may be a few die-hards tucked away somewhere) and it has proved so efficient in practice that there is at present a tendency, some say a danger, for it to develop into a yet more elaborate system from which, as a humble worker in a region in which the systematic side of ornithology still presents a certain amount of confusion, we devoutly hope to be protected.

The third name has become necessary since the recognition of "sub-species" became inevitable. A sub-species is a geographical race of a more widely spread species. Formerly the differences between these races were considered to be so slight and unimportant that scant attention was paid to them and only differences striking enough to be considered of specific value were recognised. Thus to hark back to our original example the old naturalists say that the genus of true crows (*Corvus*) contained among many others a large black species which they named the *Corvus corax*, a small black species *Corvus corone*, and yet another one not all black but grey and black to which the name of *Corvus cornix* was applied: but reference to a list of the birds of Europe and North Africa published as recently as 1923 shows us that our old friend *Corvus monedula* is now divided into several "races" some of which with their racial or sub-specific characters and approximate ranges are:—

C. m. *monedula*.—Scandinavia, Finland, Baltic Provinces.

C. m. *spermologus*.—Darker, especially on the underparts; neck not so pale: British Isles to Italy, Morocco, etc.

C. m. *collaris*.—Paler on the underparts; white neck patches: Russia, Balkan States, etc.

Two or indeed many species of the same genus can of course breed side by side in the same country but sub-species being purely geographical races of the same species occupy quite separate although often contiguous breeding areas. There is at the moment no settled idea as to what constitutes a "full" species and in ornithological journals one continually reads the most unsatisfactory "I do not consider the differences sufficiently well marked to be of more that sub-specific value".

It would seem that the only way to avoid this difficulty is to take an extremely broad view and, if the breeding ranges do not overlap, to treat any number of more or less similar birds even though the joint breeding areas extend round the world as sub-species of a widely distributed parent species. This is, however, getting rather far into an involved aspect of ornithology which is at the moment outside our province and we will conclude this paragraph by saying that in Malaysia we have yet much to learn concerning the identity and range of sub-species, so much so in fact that a number of the names we have here applied to Singapore birds are quite likely not strictly accurate.

The question is complicated by the fact that we are sometimes by no means certain to which species the old time naturalists referred when they bestowed new names on birds. The old descriptions which one must take into account are often very brief and sometimed buried in little known journals, and the resuscitation of a short and overlooked paper published many years ago may alter the currently accepted names of quite a lot of birds. It may be pointed out that there is nothing to prevent a naturalist from publishing descriptions of new species in any journal, and that such work must be recognised or at least considered by other workers, for it seems that the only way in which the synonomy of birds (and other animals and plants) will ever be straightened out is by the strict application of a rule of priority.

If a species is indicated by two names only it means that it is the same wherever found or in other words that it has no recognisable sub-species but even in this case it is usual to repeat the specific name thus—*Corvus monedula monedula* or more briefly *Corvus m. monedula.*

[16]

BIRDS are usually regarded by evolutionists as having descended from reptile-like ancestors but it should be carefully noted that this does not mean that they are in any way derived from the familiar present day lizards and snakes, etc., which are immediately called to mind by the use of the word reptile. Existing birds and reptiles have so many important structural characters in common that it seems that they may well have had a common ancestor and indeed Huxley, one of the greatest of anatomists, was so impressed with the resemblance between the two groups that he united them into one great group which he called the *Sauropsida*.

Without going into too much technical detail a bird may be satisfactorily defined as a warm blooded, feathered biped that reproduces by means of eggs and has the forelimbs or arms modified into wings or organs of flight, but the presence of feathers alone is sufficient to distinguish birds from all other living things. Just as hairs are characteristic of the mammals so are feathers peculiar to birds; the hair-like structures seen about the base of the beak, on the eyelids and on the body of a fowl after it has been plucked for the table are not really hairs but degenerate feathers.

With feathers therefore we can very reasonably begin our brief survey of the bird. Taking a broad view feathers may be divided into two groups, firstly there are the outer or contour feathers, that is the stiff, coloured feathers that meet the eye when one looks at a bird and secondly there are the uncoloured and fluffy "down" feathers which are exposed by raising the contour feathers. The "down" forms a warm underclothing and as can be expected is most abundant in aquatic birds. Mammals also have this "next the skin" suit in the form of under-fur and man emulates the example set by the birds and mammals in that he disposes his clothing in two layers.

We have no space here to deal with the structure of a feather, but it may be mentioned that the slight stickiness or reluctance with which the web of a feather is split or parted with the fingers is due to an interlocking arrangemennt of many thousands of tiny hook-like structures, examination of which is open to all by placing a piece of feather under a miscroscope.

To conclude our notice of feathers we must mention the important and usually unsuspected fact that, normally, feathers only grow on well defined and comparatively narrow "feather tracts" the intervening spaces often being quite bare. The feathers are of course long enough to cover these bare spaces.

If all the feathers on a dead bird are clipped off close to the skin with a pair of scissors this arrangement of feather-tracts will be admirably demonstrated and it will then be seen that the feathers only grow on narrow tracts (*pterylæ*) that may be likened to the paths that encompass and cross a garden, the lawns representing the unfeathered space (*apteria*). The feathers wear out and to a certain extent fade and are renewed at least once a year the process being known as "moulting": the moult is a much more complicated affair than it appears to be and we know little of the way in which it is carried out in Malayan birds.

The feathers together constitute the plumage and it is with the characters, chiefly the colouring, of this plumage combined with the external form of the bird and certain external measurements that systematic ornithology is at the moment most largely concerned.

In some birds the young and old of both sexes wear a similar plumage throughout the year; in others the male and female each have a distinctive dress, the young birds of both sexes resembling the female until their first moult when the males assume the adult livery of their sex. In yet other birds a distinct and often resplendent breeding plumage is acquired and worn only a few months when it is cast off and replaced by the duller, "winter" (non-breeding) plumage and to these three conditions we could add yet others.

[18]

Birds display, to a very marked extent, that, as we may somewhat crudely put it, plasticity of structure, which amounts broadly speaking to the popular conception (or misconception) of the overworked phrase "adaptation to environment". Thus it is that the bill and the feet of birds show almost infinite variety in the matter of shape. The bill acts as mouth and hand; it seizes the food and if necessary tears it into small pieces. Structurally the beak consists of the long jaws encased in a horny sheath. The "jaws" are called *mandibles*, upper and lower respectively, and almost as many terms have been coined for the exact description of the bill as for the description of leaves in botanical parlance. A bill may be turgid, long, epignathous, dentirostral or a host of other things, each of these words being but one of a series designed to express a certain set of conditions, but with these we are not particularly interested.

A moment's thought will call to mind any number of bill modifications admirably suited for the work they have to perform: the waders for instance have a long, thin bill well suited to probing in the soft mud, the owls and hawks strong hooked weapons very appropriate to birds of rapacious habits and the ducks have an excellent instrument for straining food from the water.

The legs and feet again show great variety in shape and relative size. In ground-living birds such as the ostriches, bustards and game-birds they are large and strong but in birds of marked aerial habits such as the swallows, swifts and night jars they have become very small. In fact quite as much diversity is shown as in the bill. The perching-birds have three toes in front and one behind—a very convenient device for grasping boughs. The zygodactyle or yoke-toed foot of the woodpeckers, the webbed feet of aquatic birds and the aggressive heavily armed feet of the eagles are but a few of the leading modifications of the avian foot. A bird is of course digitigrade; that is to say it walks on its toes and not on the flat of the foot as does man. It follows that the joints of the birds legs usually referred to as "ankle" and "knee" are really "base of the toes" and "ankle" the true knee being well up near the body and covered with feathers. Contrary to expectation then, the long shank-like bone or "leg" in the bird does not in any way represent the shin of the man but his "instep". This shank-like bone is known in ornithology as the tarsus although from the point of view of the comparative anatomist it is really rather more than the tarsus.

The wing seems to have been evolved from a forelimb that was used in the ambulatory manner common to quadrupeds. It consists of a series of bones, corresponding very closely to those in our own hand, wrist and arm, to which are attached the large flight feathers or quills. The quills that grow from the bones of the hand are known as primaries and those attached to the forearm (ulna) are called secondaries. Both above and below the bases of the quills are strengthened by series of small, neatly arranged feathers—the upper and lower wing-coverts. The "elbow" or forward point of the bird's wing is the joint corresponding to the wrist in man.

The tail consists of a series of quill feathers (very much like those of the wing) and again with their bases covered with smaller feathers (the upper and lower tail-coverts) arranged round a flattened, ploughshare-like bone. In modern birds the *rectrices*, as the tail quills are called, are arranged in a single horizontal series but it seems evident from the study of a remarkable fossil bird *Archæopteryx*, that at one time birds had a long tail like a lizard, and as in that animal composed of a large number of vertebræ. Each vertebra had a pair of quill-feathers attached—one each side—and if we imagine a telescoping process as happening to this primitive tail we can get a fair idea as to how the bird's tail in its present state was evolved. It is not our intention here to discourse on the internal anatomy of birds but perhaps a few words as to certain salient features will not be out of place.

The skeleton is remarkable for its *rigidity* and *pneumaticity*. Both of these conditions can be readily understood as suited to a creature of aerial habits. As a famous ornithologist once remarked the skull of a bird is a poem in bone—its architecture is the frozen music of morphology. It is in the arrangement of the bones in the palate that birds bear prominent witness to their reptilian ancestory.

[20]

In the matter of the senses it is probable that birds do not possess the sense of smell in a high degree: their vision is acute (the coloured part of the eye is known as the *iris*; pl. *irides*) as is also their sense of hearing.

The blood of birds is hotter than that of any other class of animals. The respiratory system also offers peculiar features—the organ of voice or *syrinx* is situated well down in the body cavity at the junction of the trachea and bronchial tubes. In breathing the air is drawn quite through the lungs into a series of membranous air-sacs distributed about the body. A bird in fact can be inflated by pumping air into these sacs, and the air spaces extend in many cases into the bones. These air sacs no doubt act as a reservoir of air on which the bird can draw when flying and it is also supposed that they regulate the temperature of the body.

Considerable misunderstanding usually prevails with regard to the various parts of the bird's digestive tract and words like "crop" are indiscriminately used. The crop is a thin-walled bag at the lower end of the gullet or œsophagus in which the food is temporarily stored and softened. From this it passes into the stomach proper which consists of two parts, the first being soft and glandular (*proventriculus*) and the second muscular and thick walled, (gizzard). In the gizzard the food is ground up, a work assisted by the small pieces of stones and grit which the bird deliberately swallows. Many modifications of the digestive tract are found in birds and it has been demonstrated that the actual manner in which the intestine is coiled provides an important clue to the classification of birds which in many respects is a vexed question.

No modern bird has teeth. Unless there is a sexual difference in the plumage of a species *it is usually impossible to tell the sex of a bird without dissection.* Normally there are no external organs of generation and even in the case of male and female having distinct plumages care must be exercised as instances are known in which old females assume the male plumage and furthermore in many of these cases all the young males wear the adult female plumage.

Our remarks on the breeding habits of birds must be very brief for we have already out-run our alloted space for the introduction.

Some birds appear to pair for life and others but for a season. Nesting usually takes place in the "spring" season and one, two or three broods may be reared in the year. A definite period of courtship has been observed in many species and no doubt takes place in all birds. The courting of the male magpie-robin on our local tennis-courts is a joy to behold. He postures and displays his black and white plumage to the best possible advantage and although the performance appears rather ridiculous to human eyes it is no doubt very wonderful to the little hen bird who in true female fashion feeds in a desultory manner at the other end of the grass court, apparently absolutely oblivious of the efforts of the male and with her thoughts far away but, we suppose, in truth really very much alert and thinking what a fine fellow he is!

In Singapore the breeding season is very extended and although the majority of eggs are to be found from March to July, the season is longer than this, but undoubtedly depends in a very great degree on the weather; eggs may be very plentiful and there may be signs of breeding birds all around us in February of one year and almost a reversal of affairs in the same month of the next year. We must omit all reference to nests and eggs but nestling birds must claim a little space.

The young bird may be born perfect naked, helpless, blind and quite incapable of feeding itself—unable in fact to raise its head in the earlier stages, but on the other hand the young of another species may emerge from the shell clad in a coat of down, with eyes open and capable of running about almost as soon as hatched! Readers will at once call to mind the great difference between the ugly naked squab of a sparrow and the active young of the farmyard fowl. Between these two extremes are many gradations, and young birds in general provide so many fascinating problems that their study has of recent years become almost a separate branch of ornithology and provides a never ending source of enquiry. Some of the differences between young birds are very hard to explain but one reasonable hypothesis that has been put forward supposes the original birds to have been arboreal in habits. It is then likely that their *active* young (as they would be if derived from reptilian ancestors) would be open to many dangers if born in a more or less precarious position in a tree. By reduction in the amount of the yolk and therefore in the size of the egg the young were caused to be hatched helpless and blind, prematurely in fact! It will in truth be noticed that generally speaking the naked helpless type of nestling is hatched from a comparatively small egg placed in a nest in a tree as in the case of the crows, etc., whereas the active, down-clad type emerge from large eggs placed on the ground as in the case of the plovers. The question of the origin of these two main types is but one of the mysteries that surround nestling birds. In concluding this very elementary sketch of birds we cannot do better that quote from Elliot Coues concerning the manner of their death. "Birds alone, of all animate beings, may be truly said to 'fall asleep' in death. When the silver 'cord' of a bird's life is loosed, the 'windows of the soul' are gently closed by unseen hands, that the mysterious rites of divorce of spirit from matter may not be profaned. When man or any mammal expires, the eyes remain wide open and their stony stare is the sign of dissolution. Only birds close their eyes in dying. The closure is chiefly affected by the uprising of the lower lid. These are the principal external differences between the eyes of birds and mammals. The movements of the upper lid in most birds are much more restricted than those of the lower."

IT will now be convenient to outline the plan on which the rest of this book is based.

In the first place we may fairly claim that all the birds likely to be met with in the ordinary way in Singapore are mentioned in the following pages and furthermore that all the really common species are dealt with in some amount of detail. The characteristic features of less common birds are noticed in conjunction with those common species which they most nearly resemble, but in some cases comment upon them will be found at the end of the family to which they belong. At the same time it must be borne in mind that this book does not mention, even by name, a good many birds that are known to visit Singapore. Inclusion of these would swell the volume to a prohibitive size (and expense) for no less than about 300 different kinds would have to be considered. It may be argued that we should have excluded all birds that are not really familiar garden species, but excellent although this course appears to be in theory it falls to the ground in practice for the moment one starts to take an interest in birds the number of "familiar" species seen every day gradually mounts up and then it is that one realizes that there are two species of tailor-bird in the garden, four, and not one common kingfishers, and that the common birds near the week-end bungalow include kinds not seen in the Tanglin gardens. Thus it is that from our, roughly speaking, thirty species of the town hedgerows we reach one hundred species without an effort—all of which can be seen as one journeys about the island on other business.

It will be noticed that the letterpress is arranged under the following headings:—(1) Description, (2) Distribution, (3) Status in Singapore, (4) Field notes, (5) Other habits.

Under "Description" will be found a diagnosis of the general appearance and plumage. This has been cut down to a minimum length and contains, we hope, just sufficient detail to enable the bird to be recognised in the hand. Technical terms have been avoided as far as possible.

The total length and wing measurement are also given but for no other purpose than that the reader may form a rough idea as to the size of the bird. The total length, or merely "length" as we have sometimes called it, is the measurement between the tip of the bill and the end of tail-feathers, the bird being placed on its breast and gently pulled out straight without undue stretching. The wing measurement (in the following pages both measurements are given very approximately) is the length of the closed wing from "elbow" (really "wrist") to wing tip when pressed against a flat ruler. By memorising the measurements of a few common European birds, the reader should be able to visualize the size of any of the birds mentioned hereafter not forgetting that a long bill as in the snipe, or a long tail as in the common pheasant, does much to increase the total length. Likewise the relative length of the wing is subject to a certain, although by no means as great, variation and two birds of similar bulk may have the lengths of their wings rather different.

Let the reader call to mind some common British birds. Take for instance some of the well-known finches, the sparrow, greenfinch, bullfinch and linnet. By reference to a book on British birds he will find that of these six species the total length is from 5 to 6 inches and that the wing ranges from 2.85 to 3.2 inches.

It will then be seen that these measurements are a good guide to the size of the bird. Anything smaller than the figures just quoted will reduce the species to something like wren or titmouse size.

We quote a few "handy sizes" of well-known British birds and the reader can find up plenty of others for himself by reference to almost any book on birds. The figures given below in all cases refer to the total length in inches and the wing respectively and are from Howard Saunders' Manual of British Birds: —

Wren ...	...	... 3.5,	1.9
Blue Titmouse	...	... 4.2,	2.4
Redbreast	...	... 5.75,	3
House Sparrow	...	... 6,	3
Blackbird	...	... 10,	4.9
Turtle Dove	...	... 11.5,	7
Moorhen	...	... 13,	6.75
Jay ...	...	... 14.25,	7.2
Red grouse	...	... 16,	8.4
Rook ...	...	... 19,	12.75
Mallard	...	... 24,	11.5
Gt. Black-backed Gull		... 30,	20.
Heron ...	...	... 36,	18

Under "Distribution" we have outlined the geographical range of the species and always broadly only. Some of the difficulties that arose under this heading are mentioned in the chapter devoted to the bustard-quail.

"Status in Singapore" needs no explanation.

"Field notes" include mention of the favourite local haunts of the birds with directions for identifying them in the field. Many birds betray their specific identity by little tricks and mannerisms or by some feature in their plumage which shows up at a distance. Identification of birds in the field is largely a matter of experience and when the eye is educated it is for instance possible to identify the small wading birds at gunshot distance by the way in which they run about. Some have a short jerky run, others pick up their feet deliberately: the common sandpiper always seems to have a smaller head than other waders of a like size and to many naturalists the identity of flocks of migratory birds passing over in the night is as sure as though the birds were on the table in front of them for so well do they recognise the call notes of the various species. Under this heading certain notice of the birds' habits naturally falls but other points are mentioned, particularly in the case of breeding habits, under "Other habits".

In no case, however, has any regard been paid to rigid adherence to a plan. As varied circumstances arose they were dealt with in the most convenient manner. In the case of the pigeons for instance it was considered that a "key" would be useful for their identification, for local sportsmen often marvel at the variation in the "punai" they shoot, whereas in some of the other groups of birds "keys" would be useless except in the hands of a trained naturalist.

The reader will notice other apparent inconsistencies. The section on game-birds is larger than that devoted to more familiar species and for equally obvious reasons resident birds have been given preference to migratory species and in many cases where there is little chance of a bird breeding locally no mention of the nest and eggs has been made. Certain more or less obscure although not rare perching-birds have been dismissed in a paragraph in order that the very popular sunbirds could be given extra attention.

For the information contained in this book we have laid under contribution many published works to which we trust due acknowledgment has been made at least to the author.

GAME BIRDS

Galliformes

ALTHOUGH the sportsman includes the snipe and other wading birds, various sea-fowl and the pigeons in his definition of "game-birds" the term is restricted by naturalists to embrace the well-known pheasants, turkeys, partridges and quails with a host of lesser known but closely allied birds such as the megapodes and curassows. These form a fairly well characterized group the members of which, ignoring technical details, are usually defined by their small head with short, stout bill and strong legs and feet suitable for running and scratching.

In the game-birds the number of eggs in a clutch is usually large, particularly in the case of the small species. If they are spotted or marked in any way the markings are so-called "surface-marks" and may be removed with comparative ease, a very different state of affairs to that found in, say, the Singapore sparrows whose eggs are so heavily marked that, in addition to the markings that appear to be on the surface of the egg, pale underlying spots can also be discerned.

With the exception of the megapodes the young of which are hatched fully feathered and able to fly (!) young game-birds are pretty little chickens entirely clothed in fluffy down and most wonderfully variegated in colour and pattern. They are able to run about within a few hours of leaving the shell.

Important as are the characters of the feet and beak and of the young, and of the eggs, they would not be sufficient to warrant the separation of the game-birds as a natural "Order", the *Galliformes*, from other birds. Such broad divisions. of the bird-world and the attendant arranging and classifying of all the known species is a matter for the specialist and he looks further than at the feet, beak, feathers, etc., although these are often very weighty accessories to the work of classification.

[28]

The expert studies details of the skeleton : he is particularly interested in the bones in the roof of the mouth, the manner in which the intestines are coiled and a hundred and one other points, but such things do not concern us here and throughout this book we will confine ourselves to those features which can be most easily verified by any reader, more especially in the field rather than in the laboratory or museum.

In size game-birds vary to a great extent, ranging from species of quail as small as sparrows to the lordly peafowl and the rotund turkey. Many of the pheasant-like game-birds (*Phasianidae*) are remarkable for their beauty : notably the gorgeous hues of the peacock, the fascinating eye-spots on the shaded feathers of the argus-pheasant and the rich reds and metallic blues of the "firebacks".

They are found almost all over the world although a few families are restricted to certain well-defined areas. Thus it is that we meet with grouse in the north only of both the Old and New Worlds and the curassows are confined to America.

Owing to their terrestrial habits most game-birds are easily domesticated and the fact that the domestic fowls of the British Isles are derived from ancestral wild game-birds is comparatively well-known. It is not so generally recognized that the red jungle-fowl, the "ayam-utan" of the Malays and a common bird in the Malay Peninsula, is regarded as the progenitor of the farmyard fowl. In the Federated Malay States the wild rooster frequently strays to outskirts of the kampongs where he mates with the domestic hens. The true Malayan domestic fowls are extremely similar to their wild cousins.

It is natural that Europeans should associate game-birds with the sporting proclivities displayed by the pheasants, grouse and partridges of the home counties and the totally different habits exhibited by the local species tends to produce the impression that game-birds are absent from Malaya. Most of the species found in the Malay Peninsula are wily birds, very capable of looking after themselves. Their skulking, retiring habits and their extreme reluctance to take wing makes them contrast very strongly with the foolish partridges of the stubble fields, the semi-domesticated pheasants of the coverts and the simple grouse that fly back straight over the guns.

[29]

It has been the privilege of few to see pheasants and part-ridges in the Malayan jungles although they are by no means uncommon in certain localities and were it not for their call notes their presence would often be overlooked. Specimens for museums are usually obtained by trapping, the traps being set by men with an intimate knowledge of the birds' habits. The chance of a shot is rarely presented.

In the Malay Peninsula are found in a wild state, peafowl, argus-pheasants (two species, one of which is very rare and confined to a limited area in Pahang), peacock-pheasants (two species), two other pheasants popularly known as "fire-backs", six kinds of partridges, jungle-fowl and a small species of quail, but of these only the last-named is found in Singapore.

It should be mentioned, however, that other species of game-birds have been recorded from the island and one author would indeed have us believe that even the argus-pheasant was at one time found here. It is tolerably certain that all these old records were made in error. Before British Malaya was well-known large collections of bird-skins found their way to Europe from Malacca and no doubt from other ports also and it is reasonable to believe that these skins were often labelled as having been obtained in the ports from which they were ex-ported whereas they probably came from many miles away in the hinterland. A large number of errors, affecting not only birds but other animals, have thus crept into literature dealing with the Malay Peninsula. As the matter stands there is no real evidence to show that any species of game-bird ever lived in a truly feral state in Singapore Island with the exception of the quail described in the following pages.

There seems little reason to doubt that before the island was cleared of jungle, before the advent of rubber and before the city had reached its present proportions birds were more numerous than at present and furthermore certain species have, very probably, entirely disappeared, but the fact remains that Singapore is a small island and however plentiful the jungle-loving babblers, woodpeckers, trogons, etc. may have been it is highly improbable that game-birds ever existed here.

[30]

An attempt to introduce a species of red-legged partridge into Singapore met with failure but this venture is responsible for the tales one still hears of partridges having been shot in former years in the Tanglin district. Owing to the abundance of small carnivores in Singapore it is extremely doubtful if any such acclimatization experiment could succeed.

A second species of quail-like bird, the hemipode or bustard-quail, is also common in Singapore and would by some be included among the game-birds but we prefer to follow those authorities who regard it as sufficiently distinct, on account of important structural peculiarities, to be placed in a separate Order, the *Turniciformes*.

THE BLUE-BREASTED QUAIL

Excalfactoria chinensis chinensis (*Linn.*)

Malay name : —Pikau.

Description : —The male is a handsome gaudy little bird quite unmistakeable in appearance. The upper parts are brown with conspicuous black bars and a few thin, pale streaks. The chin and throat are black and just below the throat, on the fore-neck, is a large crescent shaped white patch. The underparts are mostly bluish-slate in colour but the centre of the breast and the abdomen are bright rufous.

The female is quite different in appearance and is a dowdy bird lacking all the bright colours of her mate. The upper parts are similar to those of the male but the throat is white and the whole of the rest of the underparts are buffy in colour barred with black on the breast and flanks. There is no sign of the handsome white bib, the bluish-slate or the rich rufous of the male.

The iris is red (brown in the female), the bill black, slaty in parts and the legs yellow.

Length about 5½ to 6 inches; wing 2¾ inches.

Mr. Stuart Baker ("The Game Birds of India, Burma and Ceylon") gives the weight as 1½ to 2 oz.

Distribution : —India, Burma, Siam and southern Asia generally, throughout the Malay Peninsula and up to Formosa; through the eastern islands to Australia. This range covers areas occupied by birds which the systematist regards as distinct but for the purposes of this book it may be said that the little blue-breasted quail ranges from India to Australia.

In the Malay Peninsula it is common on ground overgrown with lalang grass, in the agricultural districts, flat ground and paddy fields and, as could be expected, is not normally found in the heavily wooded areas.

[32]

THE BLUE-BREASTED QUAIL

Status in Singapore:—Quails are common in suitable districts in Singapore but their numbers are not sufficient to provide regular sport to gunners. They are not often seen in the immediate vicinity of the town and prefer the patches of lalang (long grass) of the rural districts, but occasionally they can be flushed in the Economic Gardens in Cluny Road.

In the more remote parts of the island I have put them up within a few yards of occupied bungalows; and on those tiny islands to be seen just off shore from "the Gap" they can be found in the grass patches quite near the houses of the Malay fishermen. Mr. H. N. Ridley thought that this quail bred in the Botanic Gardens and well indeed it may do so but nevertheless, the only quail-like nestlings or eggs seen from that area by us belong to another species, the "bustard-quail" next to be described.

Sometimes when one is motoring along the quieter roads of the island a pair of quails will scuttle up from the grass by the side of the road and on rare occasions we have seen odd birds feeding by the side of secluded foot-paths. At these times they will usually run back into the undergrowth rather than take wing.

Field Notes:—If the reader wants to see quails he must look for them in their haunts for otherwise they will not cross his path. Some birds invite observation. It is for instance difficult to overlook the vociferous blue and white kingfishers sitting on the tops of the trees in the Cathedral gardens, or the chestnut and white kites in the harbour, but with the quails things are different. The best plan is to get out of the town and then leaving your car on the road go across open country choosing particularly to walk through any patches of long grass. Then perhaps you may be rewarded. And once you meet your quails there is no mistaking them. The tiny birds, looking almost as round as tennis-balls, owing to their very short tails, will jump up at your feet.

They will wait until you have almost trodden on them and then up and away with a whir of wings. They will fly straight away from you but at no great height, usually just topping the grass, and above all will not fly far, but when they have gone about fifty yards drop like a stone into the grass again.

[33]

They thus offer a fair shot to those whose tastes run in the direction of such small game, but their habit of dropping so suddenly to earth is most disconcerting to the inexperienced sportsman who can never be quite sure that he has dropped his bird unless he sees the feathers fly! Once the quails have dropped they run away from the spot very rapidly and it is extremely difficult to put the same birds up again. Maybe but one bird will be met with in this manner, perhaps a pair will get up at the same time and towards the end of the year especially it is possible that a covey, consisting of five, six or seven birds (a family party) may be seen. The only bird with which the present species may be confused is the bustard-quail; but although this is common in Singapore, more so in our opinion than the blue-breasted quail, it is not met with in coveys but is usually flushed singly. It has, however, very similar habits in that it sits very close and jumps up almost at one's feet, flying but a short distance and then dropping again so perhaps further notes on the identification of the two species may be useful.

The cock-quail is of course quite unmistakeable. However suddenly he gets up there is a flash of bright colour and one gets at least the impression of his blue and rufous underparts as he speeds away. The hen in her sober dress of greys and browns is more difficult to distinguish from the bustard-quail but both sexes of the latter bird show a reddish or brownish "stern" as they fly away from one (and that is the view one always gets!) a feature not exhibited by the hen-quail. When one gets to know the two birds better the slightly smaller size of the blue-breasted quail will always distinguish it in the field but this fact is not much help to the beginner.

Other Habits:—Although this species strays into large gardens and grassy patches on the outskirts of the town there seems but little doubt that it is the next species which is the most frequently seen "quail" in Singapore.

The blue-breasted quail is a rather silent bird. When flushed, particularly when suddenly disturbed, they utter a peculiar note and the sexes will call to each other with a twice repeated double note when on the ground. The Malay name is supposed, not without reason, to represent this note—"pik-oo, pik-oo".

[34]

Most authorities seen agreed that the food consists of seeds and grain and Mr. Stuart Baker adds "they also eat insects of all the smaller kinds, and feed their young at first entirely on these". Davison, who dissected a number shot in the Malay Peninsula found only grass seeds in their stomachs. The bird is unlikely ever to be of any economic importance although it should be mentioned that it is very good eating, especially on toast!

It is a sedentary species, not migrating, and without doubt it breeds in Singapore although we know of no record of the nest and eggs being found locally, not a surprising fact when one realizes how little birds have been studied here.

Nests have been recorded from the Malay Peninsula by Mr. E. C. S. Baker in January, February and March and Mr. H. C. Robinson gives July and August. The breeding season is therefore a very long one. The latter authority states that "the nest consists merely of a few wisps of withered grass placed in a hollow among low bushes and high lalang grass. The eggs are six or seven in number, dull greenish olive, faintly speckled with black".

THE HEMIPODES OR BUSTARD-QUAILS

Turniciformes

THE hemipodes or bustard-quails, also well-known to Indian sportsmen as "button-quails", bear a very strong superficial resemblance to the true quails and by some naturalists they are indeed included among the game-birds or *Galliformes*. The anatomist however recognizes that they have many peculiar structural characters of such importance that they are usually raised to the dignity of occupying an "Order" by themselves, the *Turniciformes*. At the same time it must be admitted that expert opinion is divided on this point. It seems sufficiently clear that they are closely allied to the game-birds and the only true scheme of classification is one in which they are represented as an offshoot from the "stock" that also produced the pheasants, partridges, etc. Externally hemipodes are readily separated from quails by reason of the fact that they possess but three toes instead of four (there is an exception to this rule in Australia) and this is a very handy way of identifying any "quail" shot in Singapore, or indeed anywhere in Malaya.

The hemipodes of which not many species are known, are all small birds very similar in appearance and in habits to the quails. Only one species is known in Malaya and this is also common in Singapore.

In America they are unknown, but in the Old World they are found in Europe, Africa, India, China and thence through the islands of the eastern archipelagoes to Australia where they are probably well-known to a number of Singapore folk as "plain-wanderers".

A most interesting fact concerning hemipodes is that contrary to the more usual state of affairs among birds the female is the larger of the two sexes and also generally more handsome in plumage than the male. It may furthermore be remarked that this curious reversal of the normal condition of things is carried to its logical conclusion in the domestic arrangements of these very modern little birds for once the hen has laid the eggs she washes her hands of the whole business and leaves it to her smaller humbly clad husband to hatch and care for the young!

[36]

THE BUSTARD-QUAIL

Turnix pugnax atrogularis (Eyton)

Malay name :—Puyoh.

Description :—As indicated above the female of this bird is larger and more resplendent than the male and in deference to her thoroughly advanced condition the least we can do is to reverse the order which we intend to adopt throughout this book and describe her first, a procedure furthermore recommended by the fact that it will be most convenient.

The upper parts are greyish brown and the head is plentifully spotted with white. On the back there are also whitish oval shaped spots (but less numerous and larger than those on the head) and irregularly shaped black patches. A large conspicuous black patch entirely covers the chin and throat. The wings and underparts are yellowish-buff, the former with large black spots. The sides of the breast and the flanks are shaded with pale rufous..

The male lacks the white spots on the head, the throat is white instead of black and the underparts are paler, the rufous colour presenting a washed out appearance. The breast is barred with black and this sex is altogether not nearly such as a fine looking bird as the female.

The iris is white or yellowish, the bill bluish (or greyish) slate perhaps washed with brown or dusky. The legs are very like the beak in colour.

Although to be expected it is interesting to note that young females, *i.e.* before they have assumed the adult plumage, are much more like the adult male than the grown-up members of their own sex. They entirely lack the black chin and throat.

In a pair that we recently measured, the female was $6\frac{1}{2}$ inches in length and the male $5\frac{3}{4}$ inches. The wing is between 3 and $3\frac{1}{2}$ inches long.

In weight there seems to be little to choose between the male bustard-quail and both sexes of the blue-breasted quail, but females of the former apparently run a little heavier. The species are so near in size that there is not much to choose between them.

Distribution:—In any attempt to give the distribution of this bird in popular parlance a problem at once presents itself and the difficulty will frequently recur throughout this book. Strictly speaking, the actual "kind" of bustard-quail found in Singapore is somewhat limited in range for it is only a geographical race of a more widely spread species and ideas as to what constitutes a "species" are by no means settled.

All that we can do, without going into technical details and employing the jargon of serious ornithologists, is to take a broad view of each case as it occurs and although in some cases the result will not be strictly accurate from a scientific point of view, it will be of more value to the student for whom the book was written than any more detailed exposition.

To define the limits of the actual sub-species of any bird as found in Singapore would create quite a wrong impression because in a good number of cases the actual race found in the south of the Malay Peninsula is comparatively restricted in range whereas to all intents and purposes the bird may be common throughout the whole of southern Asia and perhaps even enjoy a range practically cosmopolitan!

It is possible that it will be remarked that this difficulty could have been obviated by giving the range of the bird as indicated by its second or "specific" name.

The objection to this is that very few ornithologists are agreed as to what are the limits of a species. The present writer takes a very wide view and would unite many birds, sometimes common to both America and the Old World, contending that although the distance separating them may be many thousands of miles they are just as much sub-species, geographical races, local forms or anything else one may care to call them as the very slightly altered island forms found in many an archipelago.

[38]

In this book therefore we shall judge each case on its merits (an unsatisfactory method it is true for one who by preference works with a large scale map and a millimetre rule but apparently the only course left open).

To go back to a consideration of the geographical range of our bustard-quail which matter was occupying our attention when the above dissertation intruded itself, we find that the bird found in the Malay Peninsula is only very slightly different from that occupying the greater part of India and Ceylon: to the man in the street they are one and the same bird. Thus we will consider the range as extending from Ceylon, through India, Burma, Siam, China, Formosa, and in the south through the Malay Peninsula to Java and Sumatra—but not Borneo!

In the Malay Peninsula it is a common bird, like the quail preferring the open spaces and lalang patches.

Status in Singapore:—The Bustard-quail is common in Singapore being found in situations similar to those inhabited by the blue-breasted quail. Like this latter species it is not a conspicuous bird, and it would be easy to live a life-time on the island without seeing one although people who take their walks over the country-side are certain to meet with some.

In Singapore it appears to be more numerous than the blue-breasted quail. Kelham (1882) wrote: "Among the 'lalang' grass round the barracks at Singapore, Bustard Quail were very common". At the present day it would scarcely be accurate to say that they are very common near the barracks but they are still to be found there and a few pairs still breed close by in the Botanic Gardens.

Field Notes:—The normal behaviour of this bird, under the circumstances with which one meets with it in Singapore has already been sufficiently described above under the heading of the blue-breasted quail. Suffice it to say that like that bird it is usually seen when walking across grass land. It sits close, flying up off the ground almost in front of one and after a short, low flight tumbles very abruptly into the grass after which it is difficult to put up a second time. As the bird flies away from one, or more particularly at the moment when it jumps up, the bright rufous patches on the sides of its body form a characteristic rear-lamp revealing the owner's identity.

Bustard-quails are usually flushed singly and fly very fast. In the grass they are often extremely difficult to flush, running with great rapidity and trusting to their legs rather than to their wings as a means of escape, even in the presence of dogs. They fly straight enough but the sportsman must be quick with his gun to bring them down.

Other habits:—There are few birds in Singapore whose domestic economy would so thoroughly repay a diligent and exhaustive enquiry on the part of a naturalist as the bustard-quail, and the job is confidently recommended to the tyro not only for the interesting observations that would accrue, but also for the most excellent training it would provide in patient bird-watching. In the bird-world the work of building the nest, of sitting on the eggs until they are hatched and of feeding the young is very frequently shared by the sexes, but in some cases the hen bird alone is made responsible for these duties.

Only in a few cases is the sexual role reversed by the male alone undertaking the work, and it is especially to be noted that the instances occur among birds of very widely separated families. Very few cases of this phenomenon have been recorded and curiously enough two of them occur in Malaya. With the Painted Snipe (*Rostratula capensis*) we are not concerned for although it has, in the past, been recorded from Singapore, it certainly does not breed here, but the other Malayan species of these peculiar habits, the bustard-quail, is quite numerous in Singapore.

It is easy to understand that this reversal of the more usual state of affairs gives rise to much thought and speculation particularly as to its origin, and any observations on the breeding habits of hemipodes are therefore of great value.

A period of courtship is commonly to be noticed among birds. The males, usually more handsomely coloured and often presenting bizarre and wonderful "secondary sexual characters" in the way of gorgeous plumage, elaborate crests, tails and frills, etc. compete with each other for the more plainly coloured hens. In some instances regular tournaments take place and it seems evident that the superior song of the cock

[40]

bird of those species whose voice is their chief asset in the courtship period is also designed for the purpose of attracting the female. These beautiful songsters, be it noted, are more often than not clad in a dingy livery very different from the brilliant plumage of the songless birds.

We are not altogether surprised therefore when we find that where the male alone broods the eggs and rears the young it is the female which is the larger, handsomer sex and furthermore, the observations available seem to indicate most conclusively, that not only has she assumed the mantle of the male with regard to dress but that in doing so she has acquired the male character with such a thoroughness that she deliberately woos her small partner to be and is pugnacious in disposition!

Mr. W. P. Pycraft ("A History of Birds") says: "A recent writer, Mr. D. Seth-Smith has added much to our knowledge of this matter from his observation on captive species of the Australian Hemipode (*Turnix varia*). The courting of the female recalls that of the male of the Common Pigeon, the crop being inflated with air, the while the proud suitor bows and 'coos' to her chosen mate. He describes the courting thus: .... 'The male squats upon the ground amongst short grass and the female runs round him in a circle with tail more or less erected and crop puffed out. She then stops and faces him and commences 'booming' or 'cooing' to him......the while stamping and scratching on the ground with her feet. The male meanwhile answers her with low crooning notes. At this time the female would very frequently pick up a dainty morsel, such as a grub or grain of seed, and holding it at the tip of her bill, would call her mate and present it to him. So soon as all the eggs were laid the cock commenced to sit, and the hen took no more notice of him, but commenced to boom as if to call another mate.' "

The above facts seem to indicate that hemipodes are polyandrous, a conclusion supported by other naturalists.

Legge in his "Birds of Ceylon" writes: "Some of the Bustard Quails.........are remarkable for the Amazonian disposition of the females, which, being larger and more handsomely plumaged than their partners, exhibit, during the breeding season particularly, the bold and combative propensities which usually characterize the males. The hen birds attract each other by uttering their note, which Jerdon aptly styles a 'purring call'; and when a *rencontre* takes place they at once engage in combat. So intent are they in carrying on the battle that I have stopped my carriage within a few yards of a pair fighting by the roadside in the 'cinnamon' and watched them for some time without their taking any notice of me!"

Mr. Stuart Baker, a much more recent authority, states that he has kept several species of bustard-quail in captivity, "but I found that though I could keep any numbers of the males together, I could not keep two females, as they always fought until one was disabled. Unfortunately I never managed to induce them to breed, though the hens would drop casual eggs here and there, of which they took no notice.

"It is the cock bird that has to do all the hatching and looking after the young, and the hen, as soon as she has laid her first set of eggs, goes off to hunt up another male to look after her second, and so on, until matrimony palls for the season, and she either indulges in lonely blessedness or joins one or two other ladies who are also grass widows for the time being.

"The male, having hatched the eggs, a process which takes about twelve days, then looks after the young and brings them up, performing his duties in the most admirable manner, feeding, tending them with the greatest solicitude, brooding them at night and fighting for them against all possible enemies, sometimes, including their mother, with the greatest bravery.

"Whether, when in a state of freedom, having brought up one family, he thereupon undertakes the duties of a second it is impossible to say; but in captivity, when he is the only gentleman available, the lady generally enforces these duties upon him, at least twice, if not more often."

[42]

Hume, one of the greatest ornithologists who ever lived, aptly remarked: "Almost throughout the higher sections of the animal kingdom you have the males fighting for the females, the females caring for the young: here, in one insignificant little group of tiny birds, you have the ladies fighting duels to preserve the chastity of their husbands, and these latter sitting meekly in the nursery and tending the young."

It is many years since these words were written and since then we have learnt much but even now there is a lot to be cleared up with reference to the hemipodes' habits. May be the somewhat amusing native belief (Indian) quoted by Hume has a solid foundation—"as soon as the clutch [*i.e.* the set of eggs] is complete, the female drives the reluctant male on to the eggs, and thereafter gives·him a tremendous thrashing if ever she catches him away from these............ . True, an old Mughul Shikári, whom I employed when I was in the Meerut district, used to aver that he had often watched the males feeding near their nests rush on to the eggs at the sound of the female's call, and sit there, looking as if they had not left the nest for at least a week, until the female appeared, walked once or twice round the nest, and strutted off again, calling vociferously, as much as to say 'Lucky for you it's all right, my little friend!' But this old ruffian was one who held that : —

'A spaniel, a woman, a walnut tree,
The more you whap'em the better they be;'

and these reminiscences of his, chiefly narrated (and perhaps concocted) in view to impressing on my youthful mind a wholesome lesson as to the lengths to which the female sex, if not kept under proper restraint, is apt to stray, must assuredly be set down as 'requiring confirmation.' "

The Malays take advantage of the pugnacious habits of the hens and have an ingenious trap within which one bird is placed as a decoy. The wild females enter the trap to give combat to the decoy-bird and are caught.

In conclusion we may state that the eggs which are usually four in number and are "pale-greyish olive, thickly spotted with brownish olive and brown, the markings being often more densely congregated at one end, forming a zone", are deposited in a mere apology for a nest in the grass on the ground.

The nestlings are tiny balls of fluffy down, pale below but brown above with markings both lighter and darker than the ground colour.

The breeding season in Singapore appears to be from May to July.

The bustard-quail seems to be a very silent bird although in the breeding season the females call to the male with a note which is best described as a soft booming and which without doubt has a ventriloquial effect.

The food, like that of the blue-breasted quail, consists of seeds and insects and like this latter bird the bustard-quail is a toothsome morsel on toast although we should prefer ours to be obtained in a locality where they are more numerous and therefore more easily to be spared from the country-side than in Singapore.

PIGEONS

Columbiformes

THE pigeons as a group are extremely well defined. In the words of Ogilvie-Grant, formerly in charge of the department of birds at the British Museum of Natural History, "the birds of this order possess so characteristic a physiognomy that they may be easily recognised at the first glance" and indeed their short rather feeble beaks with the naked swollen skin at the base and the well-known contour of their bodies render it unnecessary for us to write more of their physical characteristics.

Anatomically they are closely related to the game-birds and also to the sand-grouse.

Young pigeons, which when just hatched are blind and naked although they rapidly develop a coat of long thin down, are fed by their parents with a fluid secreted in the crop. "Pigeon's milk" is therefore not entirely fabulous.

The nest is a very poor affair, often amounting to little more than a rough platform of twigs always containing pure white eggs, usually two in number.

The extinct Dodo and the Solitaire were large pigeons which had lost the power of flight, a circumstance no doubt due to the fact that they lived on the small islands of Mauritius and Rodriguez where food was plentiful and enemies scarce and the necessity for flying much reduced.

Several hundreds of species are known and they are found all over the world. They are particularly abundant in the East and in Australia and many species are esteemed as food.

In Malaya more than twenty different kinds of pigeon are found. This includes a number not known from Singapore. Such are the ground-loving Nicobar pigeon, a metallic-green bird with long hackles on its neck, which does not live on the mainland but prefers the small islands near the coast; a bulky "imperial pigeon" very much like the "pergam" of the Malays but coppery rather than green in plumage; a large green pigeon with a very thick bill, a true denizen of the jungle; certain long-tailed green pigeons (*Sphenocercus*), two Cuckoo-doves (*Macropygia*) and one or two others.

The author's list of Singapore birds contains the names of no less than ten different pigeons and unlike some of the birds listed therein all of these have a fair claim to be included in the Singapore avifauna, for of nine of them freshly killed specimens have been examined and the tenth certainly occurs as we have seen specimens in various localities on the island. The situation therefore calls for drastic treatment if this book is to be kept within reasonable limits and a few of the species less likely to be met with must be dismissed in a few lines.

Drawn by G. A. Levett-Yeats.

THE COMMON GREEN PIGEON.

Treron vernans.

THE COMMON OR PINK-NECKED GREEN PIGEON

Treron vernans vernans (Linn.)

Malay name:—Punai.

Description:—The male and the female differ somewhat markedly in plumage. The male has the head grey and a broad purplish-lilac collar round the neck. The upper parts are green tinged with brownish on the upper tail coverts. A large orange patch is conspicuous on the breast which is otherwise green like the back. The abdomen is greenish yellow and the under-tail coverts chestnut. Excepting the quills which are black, the wings are green crossed diagonally by a narrow yellow bar. Seen from above the tail is slaty-blue with a black tip.

The female has the head green and she never develops the bright orange patch on the breast or the lilac collar. The underparts are much lighter and not so deep a green as in the male, and the under-tail coverts instead of being deep chestnut are yellowish-white faintly tinged here and there with pale chestnut.

Until they moult in their first autumn when the adult plumage is gradually acquired, the young males are very similar in plumage to the adult females.

The horny part of the beak is slaty in colour but the soft basal portion is greenish. The legs are red or purplish.

The length is given by some good authorities as reaching 11 inches but most of the birds measured by us are nearer 9½ inches; wing between 5 and 6 inches. There is very little difference in size between the sexes.

Distribution:—This punai is not found in India proper, the "green pigeons" of that country being of allied species, but broadly speaking its geographical range extends from Siam, through the Malay Peninsula to Sumatra, Borneo, Java, Celebes and the Philippines. In the Peninsula it is very numerous and the commonest of the small green pigeons collectively known as "punai" although the more observant of Malays and sportsmen indicate that they recognise the specific differences of the several allied and common species by their use of the vernacular "punai daun", "punai siul" and "punai bakau". Of these we have more to say below.

Status in Singapore : —This pigeon is common in Singapore and at certain seasons the small swiftly-flying flocks must be familiar to all residents, even those living in the immediate environs of the town. It breeds on the island and is also abundant on the smaller islands in the Johore Straits and to the south of Singapore. Even to this day a hundred or so may be seen on some evenings from a point as near the town as the Botanic Gardens, but there seems little room to doubt that, locally at least, the punai has decreased very much in numbers during recent years. It is a resident bird and not migratory in the true sense, but if not breeding its presence in any numbers is more often than not to be associated with the fruiting of certain trees.

In former years enormous bags could be obtained in or near Singapore and a hundred or two birds from one evening's "shoot" does not appear to have been exceptional, but in the words of Singapore's oldest sportsman, Mr. G. P. Owen, "The days of sport on the island are almost over, and one cannot but regret that the all-conquering rubber has put an end to one of the most delightful pastimes which our predecessors of as recently as twenty years ago thoroughly enjoyed".

Odd pigeons sometimes stray into the town gardens but they are normally only met with on the outskirts of the town and are naturally most abundant further afield.

Field Notes : —Small flocks of pigeons seen in or near Singapore are usually of this species and when anywhere near the town itself almost certainly so. The observer will almost invariably see them either flighting in the evening, or feeding or resting in tall trees. Under the former circumstances they cannot be mistaken, for the flocks of birds usually appear about an hour before sunset, flock after flock following the same route passing over certain landmarks with wonderful

[48]

precision until dark and this regular procession may be seen for many evenings in succession. They will never be seen on the ground like the three doves of which more anon and in Singapore can only be confused in the field with certain other kinds of punai.

We have at various times examined with binoculars a number of green pigeons feeding in the tall trees of the Botanic Gardens and feel certain that they are always *Treron vernans* and not these other allied species which appear to have their own particular haunts.

In the case of the males of *vernans* with their bright orange breasts no mistake is possible, but the females of all the small green pigeons likely to be met with locally are extremely similar in plumage. At the same time it may be remarked that mixed flocks do not seem to occur hereabouts and the possibility of confusion is therefore removed. In flight the punai appears about two-thirds the size of the heavy domestic pigeons kept locally.

Other habits:—The punai is a bird of extremely regular habits and its daily doings seem to be governed by rules almost as inflexible as those of the sea-fowl on the marshes at home.

The squab is hatched from a pure white egg which unlike many white eggs has no great amount of polish or gloss. Two eggs are laid in a rough nest of dry twigs. The only nest we have seen was on an island near Singapore in the month of April. It was in a bush about five feet from the ground but unfortunately, and very carelessly, at the time we did not take special note as to whether the nest was built actually in the bush or whether it was attached to the tall fern fronds growing around and also quite through the bush. This is rather an interesting point to which attention should be paid when nests are found. This kind of situation seems to be the usual one for a nest, for unlike many other pigeons the punai does not select the higher parts of tall trees for building purpose and the nests always seem to be placed from about five to ten feet only above the ground.

Mr. H. C. Robinson gives the breeding season in Selangor as from December to March. In Singapore we are sure that it extends later into the year—possibly to June.

During this time the parent birds are seen alone, but once the young can fly the pigeons get together into small flocks composed of from five to ten individuals, and as these again may unite, flocks of two dozen or thirty, or even more, are not uncommon.

Once the "packing" takes place, and incidentally the shooting season is timed to open at about that time, the pigeons drop into very regular habits and heavy bags are made by men who watch the flight lines. The pigeons pay a very heavy price for their regular habits.

In July and August very young birds are often killed and throughout the whole autumn many immature birds that have not assumed the fully adult plumage fall to the guns.

The punai shows marked preferences for certain roosting places usually in high trees, and to these tall clumps many hundreds will fly nightly. They fly high and fast and if the wind is behind them travel at an astonishing rate. Good shooting is essential to bring them down for they swerve a lot and will twist and dip when alarmed: also they are hardy little birds and will carry off a lot of shot. They follow regular flight lines between the feeding grounds and the roosting-place but these lines may be frequently altered, particularly if the birds are much worried by gunners, a process which also makes the birds extremely shy towards the end of the season. The evening flight, which is short but rapid while it lasts, the flocks of birds coming in fast and pitching into the tops of the trees, appears to start about an hour before sunset. Once the punai have settled down it takes a lot to shift them out of the trees again. In the morning they leave for the feeding grounds and to drink in much the same manner their objective being berry-bearing trees, and Mr. H. N. Ridley says that in the Botanic Gardens they are very fond of figs.

The punai is extremely greedy and may stuff its crop so full that it bursts when the bird drops after it is shot. It is also very quarrelsome in disposition and a large amount of squabbling takes place in the tree tops when birds are feeding.

THE COMMON OR PINK-NECKED GREEN PIGEON

The punai has a very characteristic note much easier to recognise than describe.

[This beautiful little pigeon is very well-known to sportsmen throughout Malaya. Before the suburbs extended so far as they now do, it used to be quite common close to the town; and, even now, though it is essentially a denizen of the jungle and one which does not, like some of the Doves, frequent the neighbourhood of buildings, small flocks may often be seen and its curious liquid bubbling note still more frequently heard in the Botanical Gardens and the larger compounds of private houses: further afield it is more abundant.

As is the case generally with this sub-family (of which there are numerous well marked species) the punai is gregarious and feeds on fruits and berries, haunting the tops of high trees in sometimes very large flights. In the early morning from daybreak till about nine it comes down to drink and for a couple of hours before sunset straggles back to its roosting place in the tall jungle; and it is on these occasions that, if one can discover a regular line of passage (which however is often altered), excellent sport may be obtained: but it flies as a rule high and fast and dips and swerves in a perplexing fashion on sighting the glint of a gun-barrel; so takes a good deal of hitting. They are very nice to eat either hot roast on toast like a Snipe or better still in a pie—preferably cold—for breakfast. Malays who live in suitable localities, where the birds are numerous, catch them very cleverly in long nets strung up a dozen or more feet above the ground between tall bamboo poles in likely spots in short cover near where the punai are accustomed to alight to drink: as the flocks swoop down towards the water's edge the native throws a stout stick as high as he can in the air, if possible above the birds: they, frightened no doubt and mistaking the stick for a hawk, drop wildly still closer towards the ground and some may become entangled in the nets.

They are often seen in captivity and bear confinement well. Their prevailing green plumage assimilates so closely to the colour of the foliage of the trees, in which they spend the bulk of their time, that they are thus screened from any but the keenest observation: in flighting they appear very dark.— J. A. S. B.]

Allied species:—It now remains to say a few words about certain other small pigeons which are frequently met with in Singapore, although not near the town. In flight they may be easily mistaken for the punai proper and only practice will enable the reader to identify them in the field. If specimens can be obtained the following key will be found quite sufficient for their identification:—

1. Underparts largely white   —   *Ptilinopus jambu* ♂ ♀
    Underparts not largely white   —   —   —   2

2. Mantle maroon   —   —   —   3
    Mantle green   —   —   —   5

3. Crown cinnamon   —   *Treron fulvicollis* ♂
    Crown grey   —   —   —   4

4. Middle tail feathers green   —   *Treron curvirostris* ♂
    Middle tail feathers dark grey —   *Treron olax* ♂

5. Large orange patch on breast —   *Treron vernans* ♂
    No orange patch on breast   —   —   —   6

6. Top of the head grey   —   —   —   7
    Top of the head green   —   *Treron vernans* ♀

7. Wing less than 5 inches   —   *Treron olax* ♀
    Wing more than 5 inches   —   —   —   8

8. No green streak over the eye:
     bill very thick   —   *Treron curvirostris* ♀
    Supercilary streak green: bill
     normal   —   *Treron fulvicollis* ♀

A very few notes about all these species must suffice. Normally they will not be met with, but on the other hand any pigeon seen on the island a few miles from the town might possibly be one of the above-mentioned species.

The pink-headed fruit-dove (*Ptilinopus jambu*), known to the Malays as "punai gading" or "punai jambu", is not common in Singapore, but during the' last few years we have seen several in the mangrove on the Singapore bank of the Johore Strait. In appearance it is quite unmistakeable. The male is an exceedingly handsome little bird, the upperparts being green and the underparts largely white. Most of the head is bright red and there is large pale pink area on the breast. The hen bird has the breast green and the red on the head much duller.

In the field the white breast proclaims the bird's identity and we have never had any trouble in identifying this pigeon, even under the somewhat difficult circumstances under which it is usually met with in Singapore, when all one gets is a passing glimpse as the bird flashes past the sampan when one is exploring the mangrove—lined creeks. It is usually met with alone or in pairs but very little is known of the habits and observations made on its nesting habits would be of great value. Although it is met with elsewhere this species seems to prefer the mangrove areas. It would also appear that it is to some extent migratory but its movements are little understood.

The cinnamon-headed green pigeon (*Treron fulvicollis*) is known to the Malays as the "punai bakau", a very appropriate name, for it seems largely an inhabitant of the mangrove belt fringing the coasts. In Singapore it does not appear to be common but little shooting is done in the localities most frequented by it and as we have seen it fairly commonly in the islands of the Rhio Archipelago just to the south of, and within sight of Singapore, it seems not unreasonable to suppose that the bird may be more numerous on the island than the few locally shot examples that have come to hand of recent years would lead us to believe. Mr. Boden Kloss tells us that he formerly observed the "punai bakau" in fair numbers in Singapore, roosting in the mangroves in the evenings.

The cock bird is very distinctive and quite unlike any other Singapore pigeon. The whole of the head, neck and breast are cinnamon in colour. On the underparts this colour gradually merges into green on the abdomen. The flanks are grey. The mantle is rich chestnut or more properly "purple-maroon". The wings are black with yellow markings; the middle tail feathers green and the others grey.

The female is so very much like the female punai (*vernans*) that great care must be used to avoid making an error in identification. The chief difference is in the colour of the crown which in the present species is grey whereas in the common punai it is green like the mantle.

[53]

The "punai daun" or as it may popularly be called the thick-billed green pigeon (*Treron curvirostris*) is also not uncommon in Singapore, although not nearly so numerous as *Treron vernans*. We have seen a female containing fully-developed eggs in February (in Singapore) and the presence of odd birds throughout the spring suggests that it may breed on the island. The male has a grey head, green neck and green underparts. The back is reddish like that of the cinnamon-headed green pigeon. The female is green with the top of the head grey. Both sexes are immediately separated from all other local pigeons by their very thick bills, but this is a comparative character of little use in the field.

Yet another fairly common and closely allied pigeon in Singapore is the small green pigeon (punai siul) technically known as *Treron olax*. This is much smaller than any of the other green pigeons. In the male the head and tail are grey, the mantle maroon, the breast orange and the rest of the underparts green. The under tail-coverts are chestnut. The female is almost entirely green, but grey on the top of the head. Reference to the key printed above will reveal points whereby she can be separated from the females of the other species. We have on several occasions seen this pigeon in the more wooded parts of Singapore. The small flocks not infrequently get up off the ground, a habit we have not noticed in the punai. In the winter months we have met with it not uncommonly near the Mandai Road and it is common on Pulau Ubin.

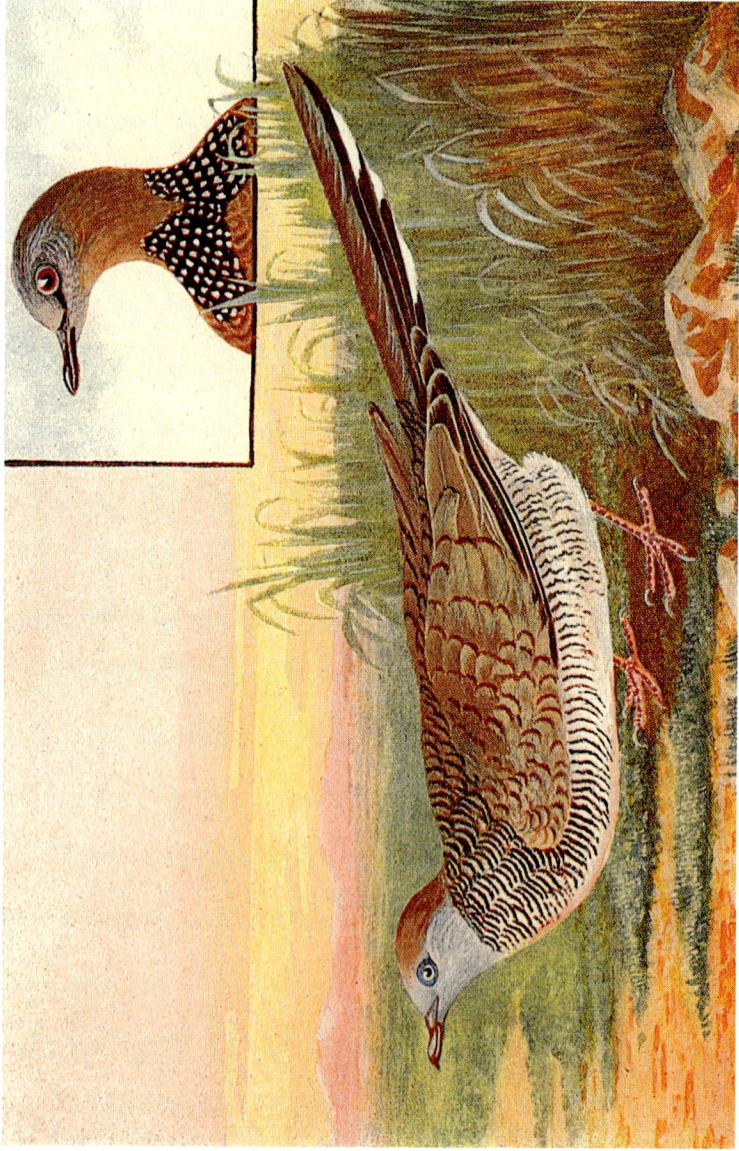

(Inset.)

THE BARRED GROUND-DOVE.   THE MALAYAN SPOTTED DOVE.
Geopelia striata.   *Streptopelia chinensis tigrina.*

THE BARRED GROUND-DOVE

Geopelia striata (Linn.)

Malay names:—Merbok; Ketitir.

We have now come to two birds with which all residents in Singapore must be thoroughly familiar for they frequent the gardens of the town houses in a confiding and sometimes almost domesticated manner, are frequently to be seen walking about our tennis courts, and most Malay syces have a tiny bamboo cage in which one of these unfortunate little birds is confined.

The reader will certainly ask why we have dropped the word "pigeon" and substituted "dove". We have in fact little excuse beyond that we are the slave of custom. A good many popular names are so fixed that it would be a great pity to alter them, but unfortunately they are often very loosely applied and indeed more often have little, if any, exact significance. That is our chief objection to popular names. We always know the bird under discussion at the moment as *Geopelia striata* and find the name quite as easy to remember as "the barred ground-dove" but people will have colloquial names rather than what they call "scientific names" and in this case we are out to supply the public demand!

Shifting the responsibility for our use of the word "dove" to another and more authoritative quarter we open Newton's "Dictionary of Birds" and read "Dove .... a name which seems to be most commonly applied to the smaller members of the group of birds by ornithologists usually called Pigeons, *Columbæ*; but no sharp distinction can be drawn between Pigeons and Doves, and in general literature the two words are used almost indifferently, while no one species can be pointed out to which the word Dove, taken alone, seems to be absolutely proper".

We may fairly claim that this book partakes of the nature of "general literature" rather than that of a serious contribution to scientific literature and therefore feel fully justified in retaining the word dove for certain of our Singapore pigeons at the same time admitting that only custom dictates our action in so doing and that like Newton, we know not the difference between a pigeon and a dove!

Description:—The sexes of this species are alike and one description will therefore suffice for both cock and hen. The forehead, cheeks, chin and throat are pale-grey, the breast very pale-pink (sometimes so delicate that white flushed with pink would convey a better idea of the plumage on the breast) fading to white on the abdomen. The back and wings are greyish-brown with black bars and the sides of the neck and body are barred with black and white. The middle tail feathers are brown, but the others are black with broad white tips.

Young birds are more barred than the adults and a brownish colour replaces the pink tinge of the breast.

The irides are white, perhaps tinged with blue, the bill grey and the feet purple or crimson.

The length is 8½ or 9 inches and the wing measures about 4 inches.

Distribution:—The barred ground-dove is found in the south of Tenasserim and thence through the Malay Peninsula, where it is a common bird, to the Malaysian islands and even as far east as the west of New Guinea. It has been introduced into other places.

Status in Singapore:—This dove is not only common in Singapore but also on the smaller islands nearby. On Blakang Mati it is numerous and its call is one of the characteristic sounds of the Pulau Ayer Merbau group. This is not a gregarious bird getting together into flocks like the punai, nor has it that bird's regular habits, but it is of a much more domesticated turn of mind, and in Singapore, at least, is usually to be found in pairs or alone, pottering about the gardens or near the native villages. It is not, we should say, as numerous or frequently seen as the next species to be dealt

[56]

with below. It is more of a garden bird in Singapore than anything else.

Field Notes:—Although this bird should be readily recognised by Mr. Levett-Yeats' plate, and indeed cannot very well be confused with any other species found in Singapore, we will follow our usual custom and give hints for its identification in the field.

The most usual circumstance under which this bird is seen is when it is walking about paths and rural roads or even in the town gardens. It walks (not hops) somewhat slowly and sedately like most pigeons and at twenty yards looks to be about the size of a bulbul or slightly smaller than the Straits robin. The feet strike one as being very short and the tail long. On most occasions it is easily disturbed and does not allow a very close approach. It then springs up in the air and makes away with a very swift flight. Just as it takes flight the tail is opened and the white tips to the tail feathers are very conspicuous.

Other habits:—The call is very characteristic and Davison's rendering "kok-a-kurr kurr—softly repeated several times" is a good description upon which we find it difficult to improve. The food consists largely of grass seeds. Beyond emphasizing the facts that it is more terrestrial in habits than many pigeons and is normally found alone or in pairs and rarely in flocks we have little more to say about its habits. The nest does not appear to have been found in Singapore although there is little doubt that the merbok breeds on the island.

Mr. Stuart Baker says "The nest is said to be a tiny platform of thin twigs and bents, only about four inches in diameter, and most flimsy in character, placed on low scrubby bushes". The eggs as is usual with the pigeons are two in number and white.

Large numbers of these doves are imported into Singapore and in the bird-shops in Rochore Road hundreds may be seen huddled together in small dirty cages. The trade in these birds is carried on throughout most of the islands of the

Malaysian Archipelago and is no doubt responsible for the presence of the species in an apparently wild state in many places which are really outside the natural range.

The Malays purchase them for a few cents apiece and carefully regard the legs before they buy a bird. Sometimes a prospective buyer may be seen staring intently into a wire-fronted box containing scores of the poor little wretches and after quite a long time solemnly point out a huddled up bird in the far corner of the cage. The inference is that he had studied the scales on the toes and has decided that the bird is a "lucky" one. Some numbers are lucky, others unlucky, but we have been singularly unsuccessful in getting Malays to agree on this point and although we picked out the older men to interrogate they seemed curiously at variance as to the amount of the lucky number. We mercifully suggest that our informers came from different parts of the country and that the required number is not the same in all districts.

Not only is the number of scales on the toes regarded as of great importance but the Malays are very exacting as to the quality of the "coo".

The bird itself is supposed to protect the house against evil influences and fire and the owner often demonstrates his affection for his pet by taking it out with him, cage as well, when he goes for a walk. Kelham writes "my Malay syce had one which, on his approaching its cage, expressed its delight most demonstratively, fluttering its wings and cooing loudly, while a stranger made it wild with fear".

THE MALAYAN SPOTTED DOVE

Streptopelia chinensis tigrina (*Temm. and Knip*)

Malay name: —Tekukor.

Description: —As in the case of its small relative, the barred ground-dove, the plumage of both male and female is similar in the spotted dove.

The head and underparts are pink slightly shaded with pale-grey on the top of the head and very pale or whitish on the abdomen. A broad black ring with profuse white spots runs across the nape, but the ring is incomplete and does meet on the front of the neck. The upper parts and wings are brown with some thin buff bars and darker spots. The edge of the wing is pale lilac-grey and the outer tail feathers are broadly tipped with white.

The irides are yellow or orange sometimes with a pink tinge, the bill black and the feet dull red.

The length is between 11 and 12 inches and the wing measures about 5½ inches.

Distribution: —The range of this dove extends from Burma, through the Malay Peninsula and then east to Timor and the Moluccas. The bird found in India is somewhat different from the Malayan bird but is clearly only its geographical representative and not a distinct species. India could therefore very fairly be added to the range as defined above. In the Malay Peninsula it is a common bird.

Status in Singapore: —In Singapore the spotted dove is abundant and seems to be more numerous than its smaller relative the barred ground-dove. It frequents similar situations to that species and is often seen about the town gardens. In the centre of the town it may be noticed sitting on the roofs of houses or sometimes walking about the roads in a very domesticated manner. It is very probable that these exceptionally tame birds have in some cases escaped from cages, but the species certainly occurs in a thoroughly wild state in Singapore and it is difficult to distinguish between truly feral and escaped examples. Large numbers are imported into Singapore for this is another favourite cage-bird with the natives. It breeds on the island.

Field Notes:—Size alone will distinguish this bird from the barred ground-dove and as it is the only brownish looking bird of normal pigeon size found in Singapore there should be no difficulty in recognizing it. Furthermore no other pigeon found on the island has a ring round its neck. It is not so terrestrial in its habits as the last species we dealt with and much more frequently seen in trees. In alighting or taking flight the tail is widely spread and the white tips to the tail feathers are very conspicuous.

It is more often than not seen walking, or rather waddling, about the grass. In Singapore it is usually seen alone, in pairs or small family parties, but in the Peninsula it is known to congregate into much larger flocks. On the outlying islands this species seems to be less numerous than the barred ground-dove.

Other habits:—Most observers seem agreed that this dove breeds all the year round. We have seen nestlings in April but as we have unfortunately never seen the nest and eggs we must get our information on these points from Mr. Stuart Baker's book:—"The nest is like that of the Indian Spotted Dove, a very flimsy concern made of fine twigs and coarse grasses, with occasionally a few roots and weed-stems added to the others. These are all interlaced to form a rough and very transparent platform 5 or 6 inches in diameter, which is placed in any shrub, bush, sapling, clump of bamboos or cane-brake a few feet from the ground, never over some 20 feet or so, generally lower and sometimes as low as 3 feet".

In Burma there are records of its nest having been found on the ground.

The eggs are, of course, white and two in number.

When disturbed from the ground the tekukor usually flies up to the nearest tree. Mr. Jacobson writing from Sumatra says "this bird is in great favour with the Malays as a cage-bird and also they let them fight, putting money wagers on the birds. These fights are quite bloodless, as the opposing birds only beat each other with the wings: the one retreating first is the loser".

The food appears to consist largely of grain and seeds.

THE BRONZE-WINGED DOVE

Chalcophaps indica indica (Linn.)

Malay name : —Punai tanah.

By giving this ground-dove a chapter of its own in this book we recognise that it is one of the really common birds of Singapore and frequently to be seen by the casual observer and thereby lay ourselves open to criticism, for in truth very few people except the ardent naturalists have ever seen it on the island. While admitting the force of this argument we maintain at the same time that any regular resident bird in the Botanic Gardens should be included with our birds entitled to "headings" and several of these little doves certainly do live in the small patch of jungle by the side of Cluny Road in the Gardens. They are so excessively shy that they are rarely seen, but nevertheless they are there. One night we actually saw a pair, no doubt annoyed by the light opera being played by a military band only a few hundred yards away, dash out of the undergrowth, fly very swiftly up the path and re-enter the thicket at the most remote end. Any bird that lives near enough to us to be frightened by our public band must surely be written about here!

Description : —The male has the forehead and eye-stripe white, the top of the head bluish-grey, the neck and the underparts of a peculiar shade of purplish or pinkish-brown and the wings and back bright metallic green : the rump is bluish-grey with darker bars. The tail is mostly dark brown but the outer feathers are grey with a broad black band at the end. There is a conspicuous whitish patch at the "bend" of the wing. The female is like the male in general appearance but differs in detail. The underparts are browner and less pinkish and the white forehead and grey crown are either but faintly indicated or replaced by brown. A few bluish feathers take the place of the white patch on the wing.

The beak and legs are red, although they are not quite the same in colour, and the irides are brownish.

The length is about 10 inches and the wing 5½ or 6 inches. In appearance the bronze-winged dove cannot be confused with any other local species.

Distribution:—This dove is found in India and Ceylon, throughout Indo-China, the Malay Peninsula and the islands of the Archipelago as far east as the west of New Guinea. In Christmas Island (south of Java) a sub-species is found of which the plumage in the male is to all intents and purposes similar to that of the bird found in Singapore but the female differs in having a bright chestnut rump and tail! In the Malay Peninsula the punai tanah is a common bird.

Status in Singapore:—This pigeon is not uncommon but on account of its shy and retiring habits it is not often seen. It is essentially a bird that keeps to cover, rarely by preference straying into the open and it is yet further concealed by virtue of its terrestrial habits, for unlike the other pigeons of which we have written in this book, although we have noticed that the little *Geopelia* prefers the ground more than its relatives, the bronze-winged dove is *normally* found on the ground.

From a study of its habits one would except that it would be one of the first birds to retreat before the advance of civilization, and no doubt this was so, and now it is only found in the more thickly wooded parts of the island. A pair or two still linger in the Botanic Gardens, and they are fairly numerous in the jungle at Changi and on Bukit Timah, but on the much less frequented island of Pulau Ubin in the Johore Strait the species is more abundant.

Field Notes:—Sometimes when all is quiet a pair will slip out of the undergrowth in the Gardens and feed on the lawns but they are up and away at the least alarm, dashing back into the jungle with an extremely fast flight. One then catches a glimpse of colour on an otherwise dark-looking bird and the white spot on the head and the front of the wing in the male are usually conspicuous even in flight. One might walk along the narrow footpath in the Gardens jungle for many scores of times without seeing these cautious little birds because they slip away through the vegetation without taking flight, but quietly strolling through the gardens one can at times see them walking about on the grass, usually at the edge of some convenient cover into which they can dash when disturbed, or again sometimes one will flash past, low down, threading its way through the branches and trees with amazing dexterity. Under these circumstances the species cannot be mistaken, for although green on the back and more or less similar in size the punai is never seen in such situations and when he visits the Gardens it is always in small swiftly flying flocks that pass over well up in the air or settle in the tops of the tall trees.

Other habits:—Writing of this bird in the Malay Peninsula Mr. H. C. Robinson says "It frequents, as a rule, damp localities and gullies in old and fairly open jungle, but is occasionally found in second growth forest, and I have even seen it in the Kuala Lumpur Public Gardens". In India Mr. Stuart Baker says that it "is essentially a forest-bird and, moreover, one confined almost entirely to damp evergreen-forests and their vicinity, though it may be met with less often in deciduous forest and bamboo-jungle. It is extremely partial to the banks of the smaller forest-streams and to mossy tracks through heavy forest". Everything points to the fact that the few birds we have in the Botanic Gardens and elsewhere in Singapore must have clung to their old haunts with remarkable pertinacity!

According to most authorities the nest is placed in a bush at no great height from the ground.

This bird which on account of its brilliant plumage and the readiness with which it adapts itself to confinement is a favourite cage-bird with the Malays appears to be very easily caught. Ridley's account of the catching process is "the fowler conceals himself in a hut of leaves or ferns, provided with a cow's horn and a long stick with a loop of string at the end. Having sprinkled some rice on the ground in front of the hut, he blows the horn so as to produce the cry "hoop hoop" of the pigeon. The birds come, and settling down before the hut begin to eat the rice, while the bird-catcher nooses them one by one with the aid of the stick and string". Kelham improves on this thus, "According to one of the Malacca bird-catchers, after having discovered a place frequented by these Doves, generally an open space near high jungle, he concealed himself in a small hut of boughs, and scattered rice on the ground all round him; in a short time the birds flew down to feed on the grain, and settled so close to his hiding-place that, quietly putting out his hand, he was able to catch them one after another, the sudden and strange disappearance of one of their number not in the least alarming the others".

Other Pigeons

And now, we must refer to yet three other species without mention of which no book on Singapore birds would be complete.

The "pergam" or green imperial pigeon (*Muscadivores ænea*) is sometimes to be seen here, but we suspect that the birds are always visitors attracted to the island from Johore, or from the Dutch islands where it is numerous, by the fruiting of certain trees, for the pergam is entirely a fruit-eater. Personally we have seen very few on the island but it is by nature a shy bird, not courting the society of man like the doves and it was no doubt more numerous in years gone by. Our sporting friend Mr. G. P. Owen writes:—"The pergam, a magnificent large pigeon, is also to be had [*i.e.* in Singapore] though difficult to bring down as he flies high and has strong feathers. No. 4 shot is generally required. Not far from the Impounding Reservoir a large wild fig-tree, standing in thick jungle about eighty feet high, was in full fruit, and attracted numbers of pergam. Not having any No. 4 shot, my friend D. Maw climbed up the tree, and shot many with snipe shot as they circled about. Although frequently shot at, they returned, and continued to circle about for quite a long time".

The reader who wishes to see pergam must leave the busy parts of the island and get to those less frequented spots on the opposite coasts, or in the interior where the heavy timber grows.

This is by far the largest pigeon with which we have as yet dealt and in flight looks quite as bulky as the wood-pigeon of Europe. The head, neck and underparts are very pale grey with an exceedingly faint flush of pink. The wings, back and tail are metallic green with bronze reflections.

[64]

THE BRONZE-WINGED DOVE

The pied imperial pigeon (Malay name, rawa), or as it is much more often called, the nutmeg-pigeon, is also met with in Singapore. Throughout the whole of its range which extends from the Andaman and Nicobar Islands to Australia it is never found far from the coasts and in the Malay Peninsula is rigidly confined to the small islands near the coast and the mangrove. In Singapore it is sometimes to be found along the coast of the western half of the island, but its occurrence in numbers depends on the fruiting of certain trees and it is rarely safe to count on seeing this beautiful bird in any one locality at a specified time. We have seen nutmeg-pigeons in small flocks on the tiny Pulau Merambong off the W. coast of Singapore and also on the coast of Tuas on the mainland of Singapore in the month of August. The birds were extremely shy. They were feeding on the fruit of very tall trees and look flight on the least alarm. We managed to get one or two by waiting at the foot of the tree from which they were originally disturbed until they returned to feed.

This handsome pigeon is unique in appearance being entirely black and white. The head, body and wings are white and the wing-quills and the terminal half of the tail are black. A very rare pigeon known as *Columba argentina* and which may popularly be called the silver-pigeon may possibly be recorded from Singapore in the future. It is extremely like the nutmeg-pigeon in appearance but has the white of that bird replaced by delicate grey. Any bags of nutmeg-pigeon obtained locally should be carefully examined in view of the possible occurrence of the much rarer species. Both these species are much larger than the punai and rival the domesticated pigeon in size.

RAILS

Ralliformes

THE rail-like birds are familiar to most Europeans on account of the fact that they are well represented in most parts of the British Isles by the coot, moorhen, water-rail and corncrake.

In Malaya are found examples of both the families into which the Order is divided. With the finfoots, however, we are not concerned. They are curious aberrant birds closely related to the more typical rails but somewhat like a grebe in form. Finfoots are found on certain rivers in the Malay Peninsula but do not occur in Singapore. Excluding these little-known birds, for not much has been recorded of their habits, eleven rail-like birds are known from Malaya. Of these no less than eight have been recorded from Singapore although only the two species dealt with below are anything like common. The absentees from Singapore are the purple coot (*Porphyrio*) and two small "crakes". The common coot, curiously enough, does not occur in the Malay Peninsula but is known from Sumatra.

On handling the body of a dead rail, particularly one of the true rails, the least observant of persons will surely remark its curious contour. The body is compressed from side to side, *i.e.*, laterally compressed, and the concave wings are very closely fitting. The legs and toes are rather long, the latter often exceptionally so, and the bird is altogether admirably fitted for the life it leads.

Rails are normally birds of the swamps and river banks, the fens and grassy places. They have skulking, retiring habits and prefer to escape from danger by slipping quickly away through the undergrowth or running with great speed from one part of a field to another rather than by taking flight. What better shape could the body take than that compressed form in a bird that spends its life slipping through tangled dense vegetation? The long toes are likewise admirably suited for supporting the bird when it is treading, as is its

[66]

wont, over the leaves of water lilies and other aquatic vegetation actually floating on the surface of the water. It must be noted that although the rails have short and apparently not very efficient wings they are often migratory and fly great distances in their seasonal movements.

Owing to the peculiar nature of the country frequented by rails and the ease with which they can effect their escape without resorting to the exertion of flight it is not unexpected to find that some species have lost the power of flight from long disuse of their wings and this is no doubt the reason why others have become extinct comparatively recently.

Most rails swim well and the eggs which are spotted and usually from seven to eleven in number are placed in a rough nest of grass, rushes, etc., which is placed on the ground: the young are covered with black down and are able to run and swim within a few hours of being hatched.

In range the rails are almost cosmopolitan. The plumage is usually dull and bright colours are exceptional.

THE BLUE-BREASTED BANDED RAIL

Hypotænidia striata albiventris (Swains.)

Malay name: —Sintar.

Description:—In general appearance this bird is not unlike the water-rail of Britain. The beak is about an inch long, the neck and legs long and the tail almost ridiculously short. On the upperparts the head and neck are chestnut, the back and wings are a mixture of black and olive brown, the former with white spots and the latter with white bars. The underparts of the head, and the neck and chest are bluish-grey and the abdomen and flanks are closely barred with black and white.

The iris is red, the bill reddish at the base and brown at the tip and the legs olive-brown. Ten inches is the usual total length and the wing measures from 4½ to 5 inches. The sexes are alike in colour and size.

Distribution:—This rail is found in Ceylon and thence north through India and Indo-China to south China. Throughout the Malay Peninsula it is common in suitable localities and working south it is found in Java, Sumatra and Borneo. To the east, the Philippines and Celebes are included in its range. From this area several local races are recognised.

Status in Singapore:—The blue-breasted rail is another bird like the bronze-winged dove, unlikely to be met with by the casual observer but sure enough to be discovered by the reader once he, or she, gets a little enthusiastic about birds and really starts to look for them off the high road. It is quite numerous in those parts of the island which are flat and damp, but at the same time well covered with grass or low vegetation. Snipe-shooters meet with them frequently and we have seen several in one morning within such a limited area as the flat ground on the small island of Blakang Mati.

It breeds locally. Kelham's remark that their favourite resorts are very wet swamps covered with low bushes is very apt.

[68]

Field Notes:—This is a rather difficult bird to flush but sometimes when one is walking across swampy ground it will jump up in front of one and after a low, short flight drop to the ground again. They look very dark in the air and as the legs are held out behind the body in flight they are usually conspicuous. It will always be flushed alone although several may be met with in a small area. We have put up six or more in one evening when out for snipe. Some nestlings in the Raffles Museum were taken in the month of June.

Other habits:—From *"The Fauna of British India"* we extract the following:—"The nests are pads of grass varying in thickness, in swampy ground, and the eggs are usually from 5 to 7 in number, pinkish stone-colour, spotted or blotched, chiefly about the larger end, with reddish brown and greyish lilac".

The pad of grass appears to be of considerable size for another authority says, "The nest, a pad or heap of grass varying from one to twelve inches in height and from six to ten inches in diameter at top, where there is a small depression for the eggs, is always placed in grass, rushes, or standing rice in the immediate neighbourhood of water". This refers to the bird in India.

THE WHITE-BREASTED WATER-HEN

Amaurornis phœnicura javanica (Horsf.)

Malay name: —Ruak-ruak.

Description: —There seems little need to describe this bird in detail for it is so plainly and boldly coloured that it should be easily recognised from the illustration given herewith. The plate is perhaps rather too highly coloured and the dark parts on the bird, *i.e.* the back and wings should be much blacker and not quite so green although these parts have a faint greenish gloss. Similarly the under tail coverts should be chestnut and scarcely so red as in our illustration. The ruak-ruak is roughly the same size as the common moor-hen (or water-hen) so well-known at home.

The length is about 12 inches and the wing measures approximately 5½ inches.

This is one of those rather confusing species in which the birds from northern latitudes are noticeably larger than those which breed in the south. When the northern birds migrate at certain seasons and mix with their smaller relatives a large range in size is to be noticed in the birds from any one locality!

There is very little difference between the sexes.

Distribution: —The white-breasted water-hen is found in India, Burma, southern China, throughout the Malay Peninsula and the islands to Celebes and the Philippines and up to Formosa.

Status in Singapore: —Although it is fashionable to quote that this is a bird of the "waterways and swampy places" it can almost be said that there are few places in Singapore where it is not found and although perhaps we must admit that its haunts are always near water, this water is sometimes extremely limited in extent and may indeed be but a tiny pond or narrow ditch! Perhaps it is most abundant in the swampy places but it wanders far afield in its search for food and can be seen under the most unexpected circumstances such as

Drawn by G. A. Levett-Yeats.

THE WHITE-BREASTED WATER-HEN.

Amaurornis phoenicura javanica.

trotting across well kept gardens, stealthily creeping along the depression at the side of the main roads (*i.e.* of course outside the town limits) and even sneaking through the grass on the hill at Fort Canning! It is especially numerous in the inland districts for it does not like the immediate vicinity of the sea-coasts. In the Botanic Gardens where, as elsewhere on the island, it breeds, it is abundant.

Field Notes:—This bird will almost invariably be seen on the ground. At the distance of a few yards it appears to be quite black and white with striking yellow legs. In most cases the wily bird sees the observer first and meets the situation by turning his back, a tactical move which conceals the white breast. In Singapore, however, it is not a very shy bird and indeed in some instances quite confiding and if the observer remains still for a few minutes or cautiously walks round the bird in a circle it will no doubt commence to feed again and then the white breast is seen. Furthermore as the ayam-ayam feels at his ease, he will drop that sulking and crouching poise which is at the same time an extremely alert attitude, and step daintily on his way. Then mark well the change in demeanour. The walk is slow and sedate, the feet lifted proudly off the ground and the tail raised so that the chestnut part of the plumage is displayed to advantage. And thus you must be content to watch him perhaps feeding at the other end of a lawn or on the opposite side of the lake in the Gardens, but any further familiarity on your part will send the bird running like a hare for the nearest cover. If you have adopted any deceitful method of getting up to the bird or surprise him by accident, he will perhaps take flight but will not go far, fluttering in a weak sort of manner a few yards from the ground, yellow legs trailing behind, and then seek shelter in the grass again. Sometimes when disturbed suddenly he will forego his usual habits and fly to a low tree where he looks strangely out of place trying to perch like a magpie-robin on a slender branch! The top end of the lake (near "the dell") in the Gardens is a good place to see this bird: more live in the rough ground in the Economic Gardens but they are difficult to find there.

Other habits:—This is normally a resident bird in the Colony but we suspect that its numbers are augmented on occasions by visitors from the north. It is a noisy bird and in the evening its loud raucous call or rather succession of calls (likened by one author to the braying of an ass!) is a familiar sound in the gardens. So nicely is this outburst usually timed that we always think of it as an evening thanksgiving sent up by the bird before it retires for the night.

[The white-breasted water-hen, called by Malays ayam-ayam—a term applied indiscriminately to all this class of bird—is quite common. It frequents thickets and coarse herbage and may usually be seen amongst the bushes on the banks of any sheet of water: but it may also often be observed in gardens skulking about the edge of the jungle or in the little broad sandy ditches at the sides of even the main country roads: it runs very quickly and often carries its brown tail quite upright. Its black back and white breast make it rather conspicuous: it has a shrill call. Its nest (it breeds on the lake in the Botanical Gardens) is made of weedy materials and is a clumsy structure: it lays half a dozen or more large eggs of a dull brownish-white ground colour splashed with spots and markings of reddish brown. It feeds on insects and seeds and can easily be kept in an aviary. It is not useful for the table.—J. A. S. B.]

Other Rails.

A little incident which happened when this book was being prepared is worth recording here for it illustrates, not only the habits of rails in general, but provides an object lesson for amateur naturalists.

When it became necessary to send the skins of selected common birds to an artist in order that the plates could be made it was discovered, curiously enough, that there was not a suitable skin of the white-breasted water-hen in the museum. All the specimens in the museum series illustrated some special point in the range of the bird or perhaps its age, and as not one could be spared a young Dyak lad was sent out with a small gun to get a specimen.

[72]

He was told to collect one example, and one only, of the ayam-ayam and being selfish and fond of the birds that loiter about our own garden we decided that it would be well to take a bird from a place remote from our own house.

The collector was therefore told to go and search some flat, damp ground at the back of a friend's house, situated well out of the town, until he got a specimen. For several days nothing happened but no notice was taken of the Dyak's non-appearance because it is almost an axiom in collecting that if you want a common thing, be it bird or butterfly, then that particular species immediately becomes temporarily scarce!

The public-spirited gentleman to whom the house belonged called to see us and gave it as his opinion that the Dyak was a lazy rascal for he had done nothing but sit down in one place (and smoke) for two or three days and had made no attempt to find the bird we wanted. Our friend however was quite wrong for, to cut a long story short, not only did the cunning, patient collector get the water-hen but in three days he got three other species of rails, not a bad piece of work for Singapore where one usually sees but the *Hypotænidia striata* described in our last chapter. The other two species then obtained were the ruddy crake (*Limnobænus fuscus*) and another small rail known as *Poliolimnas cinereus*. Both of these are small species, considerably smaller than the blue-breasted rail in fact. Broadly speaking the ruddy crake is brown all over, darkest on the back and brightest, almost reddish-chestnut, below. The legs are red. The other small rail, which we can call the sandwich rail, is brown above but white tinged with pale slate below; the legs are greenish. Both these species may be still common in Singapore, the latter almost certainly is, but they are difficult birds to observe.

Yet two other typical rails must be mentioned. They are very similar in appearance both being about the size of the English water-rail. The upper parts are brown, the underside of the head and the breast bright chestnut and the rest of underparts boldly barred with black and white. Of these *Rallina superciliaris* has the legs greenish-black while those of *Rallina fasciata* are bright red. Both birds have been recorded from Singapore and we have seen *Rallina fasciata* in the Botanic Gardens quite recently. It was slipping about the undergrowth in the Dell so quietly and was so clever at keeping out of sight that for several minutes we thought it was a rat. It may be known as the Malayan banded rail.

The Eastern moor-hen (*Gallinula orientalis*) only differs from the European bird in technical details. It is occasionally seen in Singapore. About the size of the white-breasted water-hen it can be distinguished by the absence of the white breast for with the exception of a few white streaks on the flanks and a white patch under the tail it is entirely dark—almost black.

The water-cock, *Gallicrex cinerea* (ayam-ayam), is a much larger bird than the moor-hen and in the male there is a very curious horny shield on the front of the head and this is connected with the beak. Both sexes are usually brown in colour but the males assume a partially black dress in the summer. In former years the water-cock was common in Singapore but very few are now left with us.

SEA-BIRDS AND WADERS

WHEN the traveller bound for Malaya boards his boat at the London docks he cannot but be impressed with the sociable sea-gulls that circle round the boat or collect in a squealing flock at the stern, eagerly snatching and indeed squabbling for any eatables thrown overboard.

From the Thames the screaming, wheeling crowd of herring gulls, common gulls and black-backs escort the steamer a day or two from port but these city dwellers usually return to land after a short sea journey and perhaps their place is then taken by the dainty kittiwakes, the professional sailors who glory in the rough weather and hover about the boat all the way through the Channel and across the Bay where, no matter how bad the seas, they can alight on the water for a short rest and ride like a cork.

Through the Suez Canal and the Red Sea one continues to see gulls and then, as the boat approaches Aden, the wharf loafers of that place fly out to meet the steamer and the ornithologist from home is delighted to see *Larus hemprichi* which he no doubt here meets with in a state of nature for the first time. But once within Malayan waters the gulls are absent and never has an individual of any species been seen near Singapore or indeed anywhere in our Malayan waters!

Sometimes small, white, gull-like birds may be seen off the coast of Singapore. They usually travel in small flocks and their fairy-like flight and long, forked tails have earned for them in some parts of the world the name of "sea-swallows" although they are more usually known as terns, and to the Malays as "burong chamar". The terns cannot be mistaken at sea. They have long, thin wings and also long and slender tails. They flit about well over the water with heads hanging down, eagerly scanning the surface of the sea for food. Occasionally there is a splash or a series of splashes as a shoal of unfortunate small fishes pass under the watching terns, for the birds throw themselves into the water with great gusto to get their prey.

Terns always seem to be full of the joy of living, dashing here and there with sharp cries and they are always very graceful in all their movements. Occasionally they may be seen sitting on the stakes of the fishing traps near the shore off the eastern side of the island or perhaps a small flock, changing its feeding ground, will pass along rather closer inshore than usual but these events are not normal. Terns however can often be seen by passengers on picnic-launches going to the islands near Singapore and indeed by anyone who gets a little distance from the land. Even between Changi and Pulau Tekong they are often seen.

Six species have been recorded from Singapore but some of these are not likely to be met with except very rarely. The species most likely to be seen is a large bird, easily mistaken for a gull by the beginner. It may conveniently be known as the large crested tern (*Sterna bergii*). At a short distance adult birds appear to be quite white but in the hand it will be seen that the back and wings are pale grey and the top of the head is black.

Our plate represents one of the smaller terns (*Sterna albifrons sinensis*) which breeds along the course of certain rivers on the east coast of the Malay Peninsula. It will serve well to represent the terns in general but although it has been recorded from Singapore it is not one of the species most likely to be seen here. Although scarcely common birds in Singapore terns are very abundant a short distance from the island. In the winter the gull-billed tern (*Gelochelidon nilotica*) and another species which may be the common European tern or more likely its eastern representative (*Sterna longipennis*) are common.

The roseate-tern (*Sterna dougalli*), the black-naped tern (*Sterna sumatrana*) and the Panayan tern (*Sterna anætheta*) are also abundant in Malayan waters and there are breeding colonies of terns on several islands within a comparative short distance of Singapore.

A small and almost entirely sooty-black bird with longish legs, a forked tail and webbed-feet sometimes flies on board boats coming to or going from Singapore. This is Swinhoe's petrel (*Oceanodroma monorhis*) and although it has not yet been recorded from the island of Singapore one or two have

THE CHINESE TERN.

Sterna albifrons sinensis.

Drawn by G. A. Levett-Yeats.

been brought into the port by passengers on ships. Any case of this bird taken at sea should be noted and the exact position of the ship at the time carefully recorded for this petrel is still considered as rare and the limits of its range are not known.

Frigate birds are met with out to sea at no great distance from land; a cormorant was once obtained at Johore Bahru and the pelican has been known to call in at the reservoir in Singapore.

Although not absent like the gulls, all members of the Anseriformes, the Order including ducks, geese and swans, are extremely scarce in Singapore and are indeed not common in the Malay Peninsula. The tiny cotton teal, *Nettopus coromandelianus*, (itek ayer; bĕlabas) recognised by its small goose-like bill, white plumage below and shiny dark green above shares with the whistling teal, *Dendrocygna javanica* (bĕlibis), a larger bird chiefly brown in plumage, the distinction of being the only ducks recorded from the island. They are rare and not likely to be met in the ordinary course of events.

We must next turn our attention to the wading birds for in the autumn and winter they are a conspicuous feature of our coasts. At the same time it will be impossible even to mention here all the species that are known to visit the island.

Sand-plovers of several kinds (*Charadrius*) are abundant and one species, which may be regarded as a resident tropical race of the well-known Kentish plover, breeds on the sandy beaches hereabouts.

In passing it should be mentioned that there is little opportunity for shore shooting in Singapore owing to the lack of any extensive mud-flats. The presence of the birds is also usually very uncertain.

The common sandpiper *Tringoides hypoleucus* (kĕdidi), also found in Europe, seems to be with us most of the year. He runs about on the banks of the Impounding Reservoir and even hunts for food along the edge of the tiny ponds near Chinese houses in the country.

The wood sandpiper (*Rhyacophilus glareola*) is often seen in the same kind of country as the snipe frequent and with the possible exception of the golden plover, which appears in large flocks, is about the most numerous, or rather most conspicuous, of the local waders. Along the shore whimbrel are quite common in the winter months: the curlew is much less numerous. Readers familiar with shore-birds at home will also recognise that noisy bird the redshank and perhaps detect the call notes of other well-known fowl of the mud-flats such as the turnstone, grey-plover, greenshank and the two godwits. None of these birds of course breed in the country and in some cases they are very slightly different in plumage from the European birds.

There is one wading-bird however to which we must pay some attention and that is the subject of one of our plates, the pintail snipe, *Gallinago sthenura* (bĕrkek; tĕtirok). The plate is quite accurate enough to enable us to dispense with a lengthy description: suffice it to say that the sexes differ but little in appearance, that the length runs from 9½ to 11 inches and that the wing measures about 5 inches. The average weight is given by Hume as 3.91 ozs.

The snipe is of course a migratory bird not breeding in Malaya. The breeding grounds are in North-east Asia and the birds come south in the winter to South-east Asia including India and the Malay Peninsula where they are, in season, very common and in certain districts provide very good sport. Kelham has published such an excellent account of the pintail as a Malayan bird and knew so much more about snipe than we do ourselves that there is no need for an apology in quoting him at length:—"Although the European Snipe is occasionally found, the one commonly met with in the Malay States is the Pintail Snipe, dozens (I think I may say hundreds) of it being obtained for one of the former. But in general appearance the two species are so alike that anybody not a naturalist, nor of a very inquiring nature, may easily shoot throughout a whole season in that land of the longbills, Province Wellesley, without knowing that his spoils differs in the least from the well-known Snipe of the British Isles.

"But if, while resting from his labours after a few hours' plodding through mud and water under the blazing sun of those parts, he will turn out his well-filled bag and carefully examine its contents it will be found that, with hardly an exception, the birds are "Pintails".

[78]

Drawn by G. A. Levett-Yeats.

THE PIN-TAIL SNIPE.

Gallinago stenura.

"The tail, instead of being of soft rounded feathers, as is the case with the English bird, has eight rigid pin-like feathers on either side, though I have seen specimens in which these stiff feathers were but seven in number. This is the most marked characteristic of the species, and at once determines the identity of a specimen; but the Pintail also has the axillary plumes more richly barred than its European brother—though, unless one had some of each kind laid side by side for comparison, the differences between the two species would probably pass unobserved.

"It is only at a certain season that Snipe abound in the Malay Peninsula: from May to July, both months inclusive, it is hard to find a single bird; but about the middle or end of August they begin to arrive in Province Wellesley and Penang Island, extending to Malacca and the extreme south of the peninsula, including Singapore, ten days or a fortnight later, though they are not found in great numbers in any of these places until later in September.

"However, it is impossible to lay down a hard and fast rule, as the migration is much influenced by the weather; but it may safely be said that the great body of the Snipe do not come south until the commencement of the wet and stormy period which proclaims the breaking-up of the south-west monsoon.

"Towards the end of April they return north to their breeding grounds; and I doubt if any remain to nest in the peninsula, though in Perak I have shot a few stragglers as late as the second week in May.

"With reference to the habits of the Pintail, my experience is that, as a rule, they are not found in any number in the paddy-fields—that is to say, when the crops stand high; and though I once, at Penaga, on November 6, 1877, in about three hours, bagged twenty-five couple on paddy-land, still it was the only occasion I am able to record; and then, I believe their presence was due to the paddy being scattered about in patches and much mixed up with reeds and coarse herbage.

[79]

"Their favourite ground is where the jungle has been burned, and the vegetation, just beginning to spring up, shows in green shoots, above the blackened soil. Another sure finding-place is rough land, with bushes, small pools of water, and moist places scattered here and there; but everywhere it will be found that during the intense heat of the day the Snipe avoid the open country, and seek shelter from the sun under thick bushes, or in the shade of high jungle. They then lie very close, and when flushed rise with a listless flight, not infrequently settling again after flying eighty or a hundred yards, but of course this is not the case in districts where they are much shot at and disturbed.

"Though undoubtedly, as a rule, the Malay Snipe are not so wild, nor so active on the wing as is the European species, still they afford excellent sport, and are by no means easy to shoot, particularly during the early morning, when, revived by the cool night air, they dart and twist along at a great pace; also among bushes it requires very quick and straight shooting to make anything of a bag.

"As soon as the sun gets low they leave the covert and scatter themselves all over the country in search of food; often on moonlight nights, when out in the jungle after pig, on crossing open pieces of ground where, during the day, not a bird could be found, I have heard snipe rise, squeaking on all sides. One most keen sportsman of my acquaintance sallied forth on one of these very bright nights: but though the Snipe swarmed, he returned without having done more than frighten them—not to be wondered at, considering how deceptive is the light of even the most brilliant tropical moon.

"During droughts when the ground is parched and cracked by the heat, the Snipe probe the buffalo-dung, perforating the heaps with thousands of small holes in their search after the worms which collect beneath.

"I think that there can be little doubt that Province Wellesley, opposite the island of Penang, is by far the best Snipe-ground in the peninsula, probably owing to its being extremely flat, well watered, cleared of jungle, and perhaps to its being very near the limit of the migration south. To a very great extent it is covered with paddy-fields, and on the rough uncultivated land bordering these the Snipe are extremely plentiful, enormous numbers often being shot in a day. One morning early in November, 1877, I bagged thirty-five couple by mid-day, and had quite as good sport on other occasions, but during the season of 1879, which was an exceptionally good one, the birds simply swarming, far larger bags were made, an officer of my regiment having bagged fifty-six couples to his own gun on one day, and fifty-four on another. But this represents good shooting; for it must not be imagined that the birds can be knocked down with a stick. Far from it, anything over twenty couple means really straight shooting and hard work, as the walking is bad and the heat intense."

[So far as Singapore is concerned the palmy days of snipe shooting are, alas, it is to be feared, gone: the increase of population and the drainage of low-lying water-logged ground have restricted its suitable feeding-places: and though a few may still be found from autumn to spring in likely spots one can no longer pick up two or three couple every morning on what is now the Sepoy Lines Golf course or fill your carrier along the bottoms by the Alexandra Barracks; as the giants of the old days actually did. Snipe shooting in the Island cannot be dismissed without reference to the privately preserved snipe-bog on the Perseverance Estate just beyond the village of Payar Lebar and only a few miles out of town: the shooting over this marsh land has for very many years remained under the control of a well-known and highly respected firm in the city and has been shot scientifically and carefully: their game book—if in existence—would, if published, surprise readers by the size of the bags: but of late years and particularly since the erection on the property of the towering wireless installation the birds seem to have much decreased in number and whereas a total of over fifty couple used to be quite an ordinary result for a morning's outing that is not the case now-a-days.—J. A. S. B.]

THE HERON-TRIBE

Ardeiformes

THE members of this Order which includes the herons, egrets, bitterns, storks and ibises are usually distinctive in appearance. The bill is long and pointed and not rarely sawlike on the edges. The head is small and carried by a long, snake-like neck : the legs and toes are long. Everything about the appearance of a typical heron suggests that it is a wading bird which lives by catching live fish and other animals for its food. Some folk would carry yet further the idea that the heron is remarkably adapted for the life it leads for if one raises the outer or contour feathers on a heron's breast it will be seen that, on each side, there is a patch of peculiarly modified down feathers and it has been said that not only are these feathers luminous but that the bird actually lifts its outer feathers in order that a light may be cast on the water. Fishing at night is therefore easy! Unfortunately for this idea Mr. W. P. Pycraft has rather unkindly pointed out that "as herons do not fish by night and the glow would be invisible by day, this theory may be regarded as exploded".

Mystery likewise surrounds the nail on the middle toe of the common heron—an unlikely spot perhaps some people will say to find romance and yet there it is!

If the nail on the long "middle" toe of a heron is examined it will be seen that one edge of it is very distinctly fringed or serrated. This curious feature has been noticed in certain other widely separated and in no way related groups of birds such as the night-jars and owls, but no satisfactory explanation has yet been put forward as to its function. The theory that it must have something to do with the toilet arrangements of the bird, the preening or combing of the feathers for instance, is almost irresistable; but surely if this is so, simple observation would have settled the matter long ago and again it is difficult to understand why only a few birds, and these of exceedingly diverse habits and structure, should possess this comb on their middle toe.

Although the heron-like birds are so strikingly adapted for the life they lead it must be noted that they are, at the same time, by no means prevented from perching on trees and although an otherwise graceful heron may look somewhat grotesque struggling to retain its balance on a slender branch in the topmost part of a tall tree, they are in fact so thoroughly at home under these seemingly abnormal circumstances that a good many species actually place their rough nests of sticks in trees. Several or many pairs of birds frequently nest together on the same tree, or group of trees, and thus form a colony. Herons usually lay pale greenish-blue eggs but in the case of the bitterns the eggs are whitish or buffy in colour.

The true storks are peculiar in that they have no real voice. The black and white stork so well-known in Europe compensates himself for the lack of a voice by making a very noisy clattering of the bill. This "instrumental music" is produced by snapping the mandibles together. The herons, egrets and bitterns are perhaps noteworthy on account of their huge appetites which are perhaps insatiable where frogs and fish are concerned and it may be remarked that digestion is a very rapid process in these birds.

We cannot leave our general consideration of the herons without calling attention to certain aspects of the so-called "plumage trade" with which these birds are intimately connected.

Steps have been taken to improve the existing appalling conditions and it is to be hoped that the traffic in the plumage of wild birds will soon be entirely stopped.

A descriptive label in the heron case in the bird-room of the Raffles Museum puts the matter very concisely: — "Attention may be specially drawn to the Little Egret (No. 6) as it is from this species that the 'osprey' or 'aigrette' feathers are obtained as well as from the Great White Heron (*Herodias egretta*) of America. These feathers only grow in the breeding season; those most in request come from the back of the bird, though at this season beautiful ornamental plumes appear on the head and breast as well. In order to obtain these coveted plumes for the millinery trade it is necessary to kill the bird, as the occasional feathers dropped by the bird

[83]

when alive are totally insufficient in quality or quantity to meet the demand of 'civilization'." In a recent book entitled "Our vanishing Wild Life" by W. T. Hornaday, the author gives figures showing that the London feather trade alone sold 21,528 ounces of aigrette plumes in nine months in 1911, and he calculates that this figure stands for the death of 129,163 adult egrets killed during the breeding season, thus entailing the additional loss of an immense number of defenceless young.

Venezuela, Brazil and China proper appear to be the chief places of export, though in general figures illustrating England's import of ornamental feathers and down for 1910, Java, Sumatra and Borneo are credited with the export of skins to the value of £38,855 during that period.

Birds of this order are found in most parts of the world excepting the extreme north but they are most numerous in the tropical and sub-tropical regions.

In the Malay Peninsula several ibises and storks occur but these are a long way (either geographically or on account of their local status) beyond the scope of this book.

The Eastern race of the common heron, (*Ardea cinerea*), another very similar but larger and darker species, *Ardea sumatrana* and the well-known purple heron are all met with, and also several kinds of the snowy-white egrets and pond-herons. The Malayan list which is a fairly lengthy one also includes the reef-heron (*Demiegretta sacra*) which is remarkable in having two phases of plumage, a white and a grey. The grey phase is the most commonly met with in the south of the Peninsula. The Singapore list is likewise a long one and includes no less than fourteen species but of these only four are at all common and likely to be seen by the ordinary observer: these are all dealt with below.

THE LITTLE GREEN HERON

Butorides striatus javanicus (Hursf.)

Malay name :—Puchong.

Description:—In spite of its small size this is a typical heron in appearance with long beak, neck and legs and on account of its characteristic plumage it cannot well be mistaken for any other local bird. There is so little difference between the sexes that one description for the adults will be sufficient.

The head, neck and underparts are mostly ashy-grey but the top of the head is glossy black. The back is covered with long plume-like grey or greenish feathers; the wings are very dark green, the wing-coverts edged with pale, almost whitish, buff.

The irides are yellow; the bill black above and greenish-yellow below; the bare skin on the face greenish. The legs and toes are yellow with a wash of green on the front. The total length is about 16 to 18 inches and the wing measures approximately 7 inches.

Immature birds are rather different in appearance being streaked below with white and brown, this streaking being particularly noticeable on the front of the neck. The back is greyish-brown and if the bird is old enough perhaps mixed with a few of the elongated grey feathers of the adult plumage. The wing-quills have white spots at the end and the wing-coverts are adorned with light spots as well as light margins.

Distribution:—Very few birds will give us as much difficulty in the matter of defining their geographical range as this small heron. As we know it in Singapore the species is found in Ceylon and India, South China, and thence south through the Malay Peninsula (where it is a common bird) and east to the Philippines and Celebes, etc. The matter is complicated by the fact that to the north of this range, in Amur-land, Japan and China the little green heron is also found as a resident bird but in his northern home he is slightly larger and differs in a few other details, and naturalists therefore call these large northern birds by another name, *Butorides javanicus amurensis*. A most interesting thing is that these large northerners migrate to the south in the winter and live side by side with our own smaller resident birds! We should therefore be quite right in including the range of *amurensis* in that of the little green heron for the purposes of this book. Furthermore, a few years ago a celebrated ornithologist at home pointed out that a certain small heron in South America was also so very similar in appearance to *javanicus* that surely the two could only be but local races of the same bird! But here we are going to leave the question before we get more deeply involved and tempted to examine all the known members of the genus *Butorides* with a view to getting the correct range of our puchong, which would be a long job.

Status in Singapore:—This heron is very common in Singapore and indeed on all the islands hereabouts. It is almost exclusively a denizen of the mangrove and is numerous alike in the sheltered creeks and rivers and in localities facing the open sea. Occasionally it strays into other places such as marshy ground near the coast but this is unusual in Singapore and the solitary bird that frequented the shores of the lake of the Botanic Gardens for many months, during which period it got to be quite well-known to visitors, is worth noting as exceptional.

Field Notes:—The puchong is usually seen alone although several may be found in one small area of mangrove. It is well able to take care of itself and we have always found it a very shy bird. Some months ago we did a lot of work along the coast of Singapore in a sampan, prying into every creek and corner of the mangrove that we came across. Under these conditions we saw a large number of herons. They would always take flight long before they were in danger and would invariably fly out to sea and never back over the land. They would keep low down over the water and after making a wide semi-circular sweep alight again in the mangrove a long distance ahead or behind us. In the former case the performance might be repeated many times in a morning, the bird never allowing the sampan to approach very close. Through glasses we could see that they usually sat on one of the lower exposed roots of the mangrove and their bright yellow legs were the most conspicuous feature about them.

[86]

We have never seen this species feeding out in the open on the mud-flats. If it is not actually in the mangrove it is usually somewhere else well protected by vegetation or the conformation of the ground. Sometimes they may be flushed from narrow drains and small concealed pools. We have seen them sitting on the top of extremely tall trees resting in such a way that at first we mistook them for pigeons.

The usual sight one has of a heron in Singapore is of a solitary bird, slightly larger than a pigeon, leaving the bank of a creek, or the shore, with a slow flapping flight: on the wing it looks quite grey, the long neck is curled up between the shoulders, the bill is pointed straight ahead and the legs, often conspicuous on account of their colour, are stretched out behind. It is by no means a noisy bird but as it flies away it sometimes utters a single harsh note.

Other habits:—The food consists of small fishes, crustaceans (especially crabs), frogs, etc. The eggs, very pale green in colour, are from three to five in number and the nest which is a rough affair made of sticks is placed rather low down in a tree or bush often actually over the water. We have never seen a nest ourselves and compile these notes from published authorities. The bird certainly breeds in Singapore for we have seen nestlings taken on the island.

Most writers seem to agree that this heron rests in cover during the day and hunts at dusk, although Blanford notes that it is less nocturnal than the bitterns and may be occasionally seen fishing in the day time in shady places. An observation of Kelham's demonstrates how unsafe it is to dogmatize on the habits of a bird. Kelham in writing of Pulau Nongsa, near Singapore, says:—"Near its shores were long rows of fishing stakes projecting some feet out of the water, on which sat hundreds of small green herons (*Butorides javanicus*). On our approach they rose in regular flocks".

THE CATTLE EGRET

Bubulcus ibis coromandus (Bodd.)

Malay name:—Bangau.

Description:—In the course of one year the cattle egret is seen in two quite different plumages. In the winter or non-breeding plumage it is quite white, but in the summer or breeding plumage the head, neck and breast are orange or golden-buff in colour. The bird is then adorned by the addition of long plumes that grow from the back. These are cast or much reduced in length in the winter plumage. As the bird is only met with in Singapore as a migrant it is therefore most usually seen in the entirely white dress. A large percentage of the birds that visit us are young birds and these again are quite white as in the winter plumage of the adult, although at close quarters a buff tinge may be noticed on the head. The wintering adults often display a tinge of the beautiful buff colour on the head and neck. In the spring before the egrets leave us, birds in the state of plumage like that figured in our plate may be seen. This is a very near approach to the full breeding dress.

The irides, bare skin on the face and the bill are yellow: the feet are mostly black although the toes underneath ("soles") are greenish-yellow. The wing is from 9 to 10 inches long and the total length is about 20 inches.

Distribution:—This is a common bird in India and Ceylon and is also found in Southern China and South-eastern Asia generally. It is common in the Malay Peninsula and occurs in the islands of Borneo, Sumatra, Java, etc., and thence east to the Philippines and Celebes.

Status in Singapore:—The cattle-egret is a well-known bird to most residents of Singapore and its dazzling white plumage and the confiding manner in which it stalks about the grass render it conspicuous wherever it is found.

[88]

Drawn by G. A. Levett-Yeats.

THE EASTERN CATTLE-EGRET.

Bubulcus ibis coromandus.

Field Notes:—There is little to say under this heading for with us the cattle-egret is unmistakeable in appearance. One or two other species of egrets or birds closely resembling them have been known to visit the island but so rarely that they may be safely ignored. Our conscience on this point is quite clear because if these other species were seen by the amateur we could give no hints for their identification in the field and indeed if the birds were not in full plumage their determination in a museum is sometimes not the easiest of matters!

[*Other habits*:—The cattle-egret is so called because of its constant attendance on herds of buffaloes and oxen: sometimes the bird perches on the animal's back, but usually walks close to the beasts and pounces on grasshoppers and other insects as well as small frogs and lizards which are disturbed as the cattle graze: it is also said to devour the ticks with which its friends are infested.

Although this egret may often be noticed in the marshes away from the town in small flocks of a dozen or more it is not extremely common in Singapore Island: but in Johore it might be seen in very large numbers all round His Highness the Sultan's Palace where it is absurdly tame. On account of its beauty it is shot far more often than is necessary and stuffed specimens are usually in the hands of local taxidermists. It is a winter visitor to Singapore but breeds in huge colonies in Burma and parts of India where it is most confiding and common: its nest is a coarse edifice of sticks placed on trees often in the middle of a swamp and some four to six pale greenish-blue eggs are laid. It may breed in our Peninsula. —J. A. S. B.].

THE CHESTNUT BITTERN

Ixobrychus cinnamomeus (Gm.)

Malay names:—Gĕlam; Puchong.

Description:—The adult male has the whole of the upper parts, including the wings, pale chestnut in colour: the under surface is much lighter and is perhaps best described as almost uniform light tawny. The young birds are rather different being somewhat browner and less chestnut on the upper parts with irregular markings of yellowish and black. On the under surface they are heavily streaked and a good number of the birds seen, even if not in this immature plumage, show signs of it, especially in the matter of the streaking of the breast and abdomen. There seems to be some doubt as to whether the female ever attains the almost immaculate plumage of the male.

The bill is yellow shaded with brown, the irides are likewise yellow and the feet are yellowish-green.

In length this bird runs to about 15 inches and the wing from 5½ to 6 inches.

Distribution:—The chestnut bittern is found in China and East Siberia as well as in India and through the Malay Peninsula and the islands as far east as the Philippines and Celebes. In the Malay Peninsula it is common.

Status in Singapore:—A common bird of the swampy places and found in just the localities liked by the snipe. Small marshy patches with long grass usually yield a bittern or two if walked through. They are not birds of the mangrove or sea-coasts but prefer spots like the low lying damp ground on the south of the Mandai Road.

Field Notes:—These birds are usually flushed singly; they sit rather close and when they jump up the long legs dangling down and behind are noticeable. They usually fly round in the air and drop back to cover again, or flying off straight and just topping the grass, drop to ground again after a very short flight. They seem to keep to cover during most of the day, commencing to feed in the late afternoon.

THE CHESTNUT BITTERN.
Ixobrychus cinnamomeus.

Other habits:—It seems tolerably certain that this species, must breed in Singapore but we know no record of its nest and eggs having been found here. This is not surprising for Indian ornithologists say that it nests on the ground in swampy places although many nests are recorded as being placed a few feet above the ground. The nest is made of short lengths of reeds, sedge or grass, etc., and the eggs which are 5 or 6 in number are dull white.

Local Malays also seem to find the nest rather difficult to find for we have been solemnly assured that if the nest of either this bird or the ruak-ruak (white breasted water-hen) is placed over the head, the wearer becomes invisible!

Another species of small and light-coloured bittern is fairly common in Singapore and as it is found in similar situations to the last species there is a possibility of the two birds being confused. The yellow bittern as one may call it (*Ixobrychus sinensis*), is rather smaller than the chestnut bittern. Its total length averages about 14 or 15 inches and the wing about 5½ inches. In plumage the two species are much alike at first sight, but *sinensis* has the wing quills and the tail quite black whereas in *cinnamomeus* these are chestnut like the rest of the plumage on the upper parts. The black quills of the former species will serve to identify the bird in the field. When it jumps up at least half the wing appears to be black.

We cannot leave the bitterns without referring to the protection they derive from their peculiar coloration. It seems a general rule among these brown or yellowish reed-haunting bitterns that when they are alarmed they stand motionless with the body held in a vertical position, neck stretched stiffly upwards and bill pointed to the sky. The broken browns of the plumage all help to conceal the bird from the prying eyes of its enemies. What is to our mind one of the best accounts of a protective device in the bird world that has yet been published is from the pen of Mr. W. H. Hudson and deals with an American species of bittern very closely allied to our chestnut bittern, and there is not the sightest doubt that patient observation of our local species would produce equally interesting results:—"...........I noticed one of these Herons stealing off quickly through a bed of rushes, thirty or forty yards from me: he was a foot or so above the ground, and went so rapidly, that he appeared to glide through the rushes without touching them. I fired.........and thinking that I had killed him, I went to the spot. It was an isolated bed of rushes I had seen him in; the mud below, and for some distance round was quite bare and hard, so that it would have been impossible for the bird to escape without being perceived; and yet, dead or alive, it was not to be found. After vainly searching . . . for a quarter of an hour I gave over the quest . . . and was just turning to go, when, behold! there stood my Heron on a reed, no more than eight inches from me, and on a level with my knees. He was perched, the body erect, and the point of the tail touching the reed grasped by its feet; the long, slender, tapering neck was held stiff, straight and vertically; and the head and back, instead of being carried obliquely, were also pointing up. There was not, from his feet to the tip of his beak, a perceptible curve or inequality, but the whole was the figure, the exact counterpart, of a straight, tapering rush, the loose plumage arranged to fill inequalities, and the wings pressed into the hollow sides, making it impossible to see where the body ended and the neck began, or to distinguish head from neck, or beak from head. This was, of course, a front view; and the entire under-surface of the bird was thus displayed, all of a uniform dull yellow, like that of a faded rush. I regarded the bird wonderingly for some time, but not the least motion did it make. I thought it was wounded or paralysed with fear, and placing my hand on the point of its beak, forced the head down till it touched the back; when I withdrew my hand, up flew the head, like a steel spring, to its first position. I repeated the experiment many times with the same result, the very eyes of the bird appearing all the time rigid and unwinking, like those of a creature in a fit. What wonder that it is so difficult, almost impossible, to discover the bird in such an altitude! But how happened it that while repeatedly walking round the bird through the rushes I had not caught sight of the striped back and the broad dark-coloured sides? I asked myself this question, and stepped round to get a side view, when, *mirabile dictu*, I could see nothing but the rush-like front of the bird! His motions on the perch, as he turned slowly or quickly round, still keeping the edge of the blade-like body before me, corresponded so exactly with my own that I almost doubted that I had moved at all. I also found as I walked round him, that as soon as I got on to the opposite side and he could no longer trust himself on his perch, he whirled his body with great rapidity the other way, instantly presenting the same front as before. Finally I plucked him forcibly from the rush and perched him on my hand, upon which he flew only fifty or sixty yards off, and dropped into the dry grass. Here he again put into practice the same instinct so ably that I groped about for ten or twelve minutes before refinding him......... ."

[The Kallang Reservoir is a good place at which to see and watch bitterns, herons and other water-birds and if one walks quietly round the unfrequented bays a sight of the little green heron (*Butorides javanica*) and the black or yellow-necked bittern (*Dupetor flavicollis*) besides a view in season of Sandpipers and a riot of smaller birds will probably be one's reward.

The chestnut bittern is called—as indeed most birds of this type are—by Malays by the name of "Puchong". It is a haunter of reedy marsh ground, standing motionless with neck humped on back and beak skywards and seldom moves unless actually flushed, or towards evening when it begins to feed: for it is a bird of the night. It flies low and seldom far, trailing its legs and bumping clumsily into the nearest brake. It is not at all unusual to see a dozen or more in a morning's walk after Snipe so there must be plenty of them. It is resident and no doubt breeds in the thickest covers amidst the swamps. It feeds on small fish, crustaceans and aquatic insects.— J. A. S. B.]

THE DIURNAL BIRDS OF PREY

(Accipitriformes)

THE Order *Accipitriformes* includes the vultures, eagles, hawks and ospreys, all these birds being sometimes conveniently grouped under the term "raptores".

In habits they are all carnivorous, but while some feed on carrion others prefer to catch their food alive.

All the birds of prey are very well adapted for the life they lead. The beak is short, stout and hooked and has sharp edges; the toes are provided with strong curved claws and by the combined use of these weapons they seize, kill and rend their prey.

The various species have very different methods of hunting. The bold peregrine dashes into the middle of a flying flock and seizing a bird flys away with apparent ease. The kestrel hovers aloft with head bent down and woe betide the field-mouse or other small living thing that betrays its presence in the field below by a slight movement. The long-winged harrier quarters a field as systematically as a schoolboy searching for larks' eggs.

About forty different birds of prey are known from the Malay Peninsula, but quite a lot of these are rare. Singapore has a list of nineteen recorded species, but of these again a large proportion will not be met with in the ordinary way and only the sea-eagle and the brahminy kite are common "accipitres" in Singapore. A few other kinds mentioned below may be met with at long intervals, but usually only as passing migrants.

Drawn by G. A. Levett-Yeats.

THE WHITE-BELLIED SEA-EAGLE.
Haliaeëtus leucogaster.

THE WHITE-BELLIED SEA-EAGLE

Haliæetus leucogaster (*Gm.*)

Malay name:—Burong lang; lang laut.

Description:—Adult sea-eagles are rather different in appearance from young birds. Old birds have the head, neck, most of the underparts and the last one-third of the tail pure white. The back and wings are dark grey, the latter with black quills. The sexes are alike in plumage, but in size the female is a trifle larger than the male. Young birds are entirely brown although by no means uniform in colour, the back being much darker than the underparts which are sometimes very pale. The breast is rather darker than the rest of the underparts. The irides are brown, the bill grey and the feet very pale flesh colour or "whitish" as ornithologists say.

The total length is about 2 feet 4 inches to 2 feet 6 inches and the wing is about 22 inches.

Distribution:—This is a coastal bird with a very wide range. It is found in Ceylon, India, Burma, the Malay Peninsula and throughout the islands to Australia.

Status in Singapore:—This eagle is very common not only in Singapore but also on all the small neighbouring islets and on account of its size and conspicuous habits must be one of the best known of local birds. There are several old nests at various points on the island, some of them, like that on the way to the "Gap", being quite familiar land-marks.

Field Notes:—This very large bird is usually seen patrolling the harbour, sitting on the fishing stakes or slowly flapping its way over the town in the early evening. Looked at from below perhaps its most striking feature is the wedge-shaped tail. In the harbour it is much less active than the squealing kites and of course very much larger. The coast near "Labrador" is one of its favourite haunts. In the evening or when they have been feeding heavily the sea-eagles pass over the island, a very noticeable flight line being over the Sepoy Lines Golf course, and rest for preference in isolated clumps

[95]

of tall trees. The Gardens' jungle is much frequented for this purpose and there is usually an odd bird loafing about there. On these evening flights they often congregate into small, though very scattered flocks, sometimes of as many as ten birds. It must always be remembered when spotting eagles that two distinct plumages are worn, that of the white-breasted adult and that of the brown-breasted immature bird, but the combined characters of large size and wedge-shape tail should make identification easy.

Other habits:—Robinson and Kloss write: "The White-bellied Sea-Eagle is found throughout the coasts of the Malay Peninsula and extends for some distance inland wherever there is much rice cultivation. Nearly every small island has a breeding pair of these birds, the nest being an enormous mass of sticks, placed in some lofty tree and added to from year to year. Some of these nests are known to have endured for at least thirty or forty years, and have become conspicuous land-marks on the coast".

The eggs are two in number and whitish in colour although if they are held up to the light they appear somewhat greenish.

According to Ridley it nested at one time in the Botanic Gardens and there is to this day a large nest of sticks in a tree in the small patch of jungle near which the eagles often settle and we have actually seen them resting in it, but at the same time we are by no means satisfied that the sea-eagles are the rightful owners. Our idea of the domestic muddle is that when the eagle's nest was blown down, as reported by Ridley, the birds appropriated as a roosting place and rest-house, the nest of a pair of the changeable hawk-eagle (*see* page 101) quite another species, and a much less common bird, which apparently nested regularly in the Gardens at one time although it does no more than pay odd visits now-a-days.

The sea-eagle is a very vociferous bird and its well-known double note, if heard from a height in the air not unlike that of a curlew although much less sustained, but very loud or "clanging" at close quarters, can be heard all over Tanglin when the birds are roosting in the Gardens. The Malays call most hawk-like birds "lang" but the term is more especially applied to the bird under discussion.

THE WHITE-BELLIED SEA-EAGLE

[The white bellied sea-eagle is a magnificent great bird and as it is of very large size and has a loud barking, or rather yelping, cry it cannot easily be overlooked. This eagle frequents the shore all round the Island and can also be sometimes seen on the big reservoirs off the Thomson Road. One or two can nearly always be observed sitting on buoys or posts just outside the harbour or hanging about the breakwater whilst towards evening it can usually be noticed sailing towards the high trees in the Tanglin district where several nightly roost.

It feeds principally on fish and sea-snakes and can sometimes be seen to seize quite large specimens as they bask on the surface of the water: it is said also to capture water-birds and even poultry and it is certainly not above devouring dead fish lying on the shore. Although, normally, its flight looks somewhat laboured its rapid evolutions on the wing in the breeding season when playing with its mate or chasing an intruding male are most interesting to watch. It is faithful to its nest and the same site is utilized year after year: if one of a pair is shot, another soon takes its place and if both of a pair are destroyed a new couple soon occupy the nest. In one great Waringan tree in a garden off Grange Road, a nest has existed from time immemorial: near "Labrador" there is another well-known eyrie and others can easily be discovered by anyone who cares to look near Changi and Woodlands. It can without difficulty be kept in captivity.—J. A. S. B.].

THE MALAYAN BRAHMINY KITE

Haliastur indus intermedius (Gurney)

Malay name:—Lang merah.

Description:—As in the case of the sea-eagle the young birds of this species differ rather markedly in appearance from the adults. The adults are arrayed in a simple dress of bright chestnut and white. The head and the underparts right from the chin down to the middle of the abdomen are white with very thin dark lines down the centre of some of the feathers. These thin lines are known as the "shaft stripes". The back, wings and tail are chestnut except the wing quills which are black and the tip of the tail which is whitish. This description applies to both sexes. The young birds lack the pure white and the chestnut of the older birds and the whole of their plumage is of various shades of brown. At a short distance these young birds appear uniformly dark in appearance and very different from the adults which, when the sun catches their back and wings, glisten like burnished copper. In the harbour both young and old examples fly together in the same flock and sometimes one can notice birds of a particularly interesting age in which the plumage is neither one thing nor the other.

The birds as found in Singapore differ slightly from the perhaps better-known brahminy kite of the Indian ports in that the shaft-stripes are rather thinner, but the difference is trivial and concerns the specialist. Further east still (in Australia) one meets with a species of kite again to the unpractised eye identical with both the brahminy kites of India and Malaya: in this form the shaft-stripes have quite disappeared. Thus from west to east we find but one species of bird varying in its plumage in a small way and the three birds can be quoted as a good example of three "sub-species" obviously all belonging to one "parent species"—the brahminy kite, *Haliastur indus*.

The adults have the iris brown, the beak pale or brownish slate colour and the feet a greenish-yellow.

Length about 19 inches, wing approximately 15 inches.

THE MALAYAN BRAHMINY KITE.

Haliastur indus intermedius.

Distribution:—Taking a broad view as to the constitution of the species it may be said that this kite is not found west of India, but it is found through that country, Burma, China, Siam, the Malay Peninsula and thence through the islands to northern Australia.

In the Malay Peninsula it is a common bird being found all round the coasts in very similar situations to those frequented by the white-bellied sea-eagle.

Status in Singapore:—A very common bird, flocks of which can usually be seen in the harbour, the birds flying round about the ships, snatching garbage from the surface of the water. Large numbers can at times be seen on the Thomson Road Reservoir and very often examples may be seen against the sky over the town.

Field Notes:—This is the common bird of prey of the neighbourhood and the large size combined with the bright chestnut and pure white plumage of the adult render it unmistakable. If birds are observed as they fly about the harbour it will be seen that, on the wing, some appear to be quite uniform brown in colour. These are of course the young birds.

Other habits:—This kite is almost invariably found in the vicinity of water, from the surface of which it seizes its food, consisting chiefly of refuse, with its feet. It also eats fish, frogs and crabs. It is a noisy bird when feeding uttering a querulous squealing note. Along the coasts it is most abundant in the vicinity of the villages and fishing places. Kelham writes: "At Kuala Kangsa, in company with crows, they used to collect at the place where all the offal from our camp was deposited, and carry off any filth they could find, often chasing the crows and making them drop any particularly dainty morsel, which was quickly picked up by the pursuing kite, though he, in his turn frequently had to run the gauntlet of his comrades".

This bird often visits the Botanic Gardens and Ridley thought that it nested in large trees near "Tyersall", although he never found the nest.

Blanford states that the name Brahminy Kite is due to the association of the bird with Vishnu.

[99]

[One of the sights which always attracts the notice of those who arrive for the first time in Singapore by sea is the crowd of kites flying and squealing in the harbour and pouncing on garbage and odds and ends of food thrown overboard from the ships. This ubiquitous bird is the Malayan brahminy kite— the Burong Lang merah of the Malays—, a powerful flier and rapacious feeder. It will pick small fish from the surface of the water or young chickens from the poultry yard: frogs, crabs, lizards, shell-fish and even locusts are often eaten by it but in the neighbourhood of towns it is content to exist on offal and carrion and is really rather a useful scavenger. Its nest placed in high trees is a fairly compact structure of twigs and sticks and it lays two eggs of a white ground colour splotched with rusty brown. St. Johns Island near Singapore is a well-known breeding haunt. It seems always in the air and though usually a lazy-looking mover—*remigio alarum*—in the breeding season or when frightened it displays extraordinary agility.—J. A. S. B.].

THE CHANGEABLE HAWK-EAGLE

Spizætus cirrhatus limnætus (Horsf.)

Description:—This hawk-eagle is interesting in that it furnishes us with an excellent example of dimorphism—the condition existing when one species occurs in two distinct forms. Considering their plumage alone many birds are of course sexually dimorphic. The reader will at once call to mind a number of instances: most species of wild ducks have quite distinct plumages for the male and female. Occasionally dimorphic forms of a species occur quite independently of sex. The *Spizætus* under discussion is a striking example of this for it is found in two such distinct plumages that it is not surprising the old naturalists regarded these phases as distinct species and gave them names accordingly. In this species the male is smaller than the female: a sexual difference in size is very common in the birds of prey.

The dark phase is almost entirely deep blackish-brown above and below unrelieved by any distinct markings. Among local birds it is unmistakable—a nearly uniform black eagle-like bird only slightly smaller than the sea-eagle although considerably larger than the brahminy kite.

In the light phase the underparts are whitish, more often than not spotted or splashed with dark brown. The head may be light like the underparts or on the other hand may resemble the upper parts which are brown; the tail has dark bands.

The wing is approximately from 15 to 17 inches.

The iris is bright yellow, the bill black and the feet yellow.

Distribution:—This bird is found in India, Burma, the Malay Peninsula and thence through the islands to the Philippines. Closely allied races occupy the Lesser Sunda Islands and Celebes.

Status in Singapore:—This fine bird can often be seen in Singapore: in fact we suspect that the majority of the *large* raptores that are seen here, excluding the very large sea-eagle, belong to this species. A pair may often be seen in the jungle at the Botanic Gardens. In 1898 Ridley recorded that it nested regularly and that the nest had been in use for nine years. There is still a nest in the spot indicated and the birds seem to be there off and on all the year round, but we are not sure that the nest is now used for anything else than a resting place or rendezvous.

Field Notes:—To distinguish this bird from one or two other large species of raptore that occasionally appear in Singapore is no easy matter but whether of the light or dark phase this species always shows a big light patch under the wing when flying. The large bird seen flying over the gardens or sitting on the top of a tall tree in the jungle is usually this species—if not the sea-eagle. The voice is unmistakable and it is a noisy bird, continually uttering the shrill scream or whistle which is not unlike the note of the sea-eagle in tone.

Other habits:—Evidence seems to show that this is a great poultry thief. A Sumatran naturalist says that of all the birds of prey in Sumatra *Spizætus limnætus* is the greatest robber of poultry but the brahminy kite is by no means free of a similar charge! It also feeds on small birds, mammals, and lizards. This is essentially a country-side or woodland hawk—not commonly soaring in the air like the eagle, or on the wing so constantly as the kite, but rather it sits on trees watching for its prey.

The nest is an untidy mass of sticks placed high up in a tall tree; it contains but one egg which is greenish white, either immaculate or slightly marked at the larger end with rich brown.

Other Birds of Prey

Small hawks very like the European sparrow-hawk in appearance are fairly common in and around Singapore during the winter months. The most numerous species is *Accipiter gularis* (*rajawali*) which for the sake of convenience may be known as the Japanese sparrow-hawk, but others also occur. This sparrow-hawk pursues its prey, often small birds, with such purposefulness that it occasionally dashes into buildings and we have captured specimens actually in the Raffles Museum.

Sometimes a sudden commotion will occur among the small birds of a garden. The bulbuls join in a noisy chorus and there is generally much excitement. Usually the cause of all the disturbance, which dies down almost as rapidly as it started, is due to a sparrow-hawk passing over.

The rufous-bellied hawk-eagle (*Lophotriorchus kieneri*) is a rare bird which occasionally turns up in Singapore. The last specimen we saw was captured alive in a chicken house in St. Thomas Walk! It is a large species, roughly about the size of the brahminy kite and the adults are handsomely clad in black, white and rufous.

The common pariah-kite is also recorded from Singapore and as it is chiefly brown in colour, it could be confused quite easily with the immature brahminy kite when on the wing. Compared with this latter bird its distinguishing features are the slightly larger size and longer forked tail. In the brahminy kite the tail is not forked.

The crested honey-buzzard (*Pernis apivorous*) seems to be fairly numerous in Singapore in the winter months.

Another large hawk known to visit Singapore on occasions is the crested serpent-eagle (*Spilornis cheela*).

A very small hawk, no larger than a bulbul in fact, sometimes visits us. It is a pretty little species black and white with a lively chestnut abdomen; this is the black-legged falconet (*Microhierax fringillarius*). Another hawk, mainly black and white in plumage, but this time about pigeon size, is the black crested baza (*Baza lophotes*) at one time thought to be a very rare bird locally. It has rather curious habits for a hawk and almost certainly migrates in flocks that pass through or near Singapore.

The Osprey (*Pandion haliætus*), to all intents and purposes identical with the species that is found in the British Islands, is not rare off the coasts of the Island. We have not infrequently met with this fine bird sitting on the stakes of the fishing traps so plentiful along the coasts of Singapore. It plunges into the water after fish making a great splash. The Malays call it the *lang siput* or oyster hawk, saying that the osprey precedes the tide as it turns, warning all the shell-fish with its screaming voice!

Even now we have not exhausted the list of the birds of prey known from Singapore Island.

OWLS

(*Strigiformes*)

NATURALISTS of a previous generation grouped all owls together with the vultures, eagles and hawk-like birds and to the heterogeneous assemblage thus created they applied the term "birds of prey" or "raptores". The raptores they divided into the diurnal birds of prey and the nocturnal birds of prey, the latter division of course including the owls. The harriers were supposed to represent a link between the two groups. In external appearance there are certainly many points of likeness between an owl and a hawk. Both have the strong curved beak and well-bent, cruel talons; but later research, chiefly anatomical, showed that the early classifiers were wrong and that with the superficial resemblance mentioned above the relation between the accipitres, as we now call the diurnal raptores, and the owls was ended.

The general appearance of a typical owl is familiar to most people. The "face" is curiously flat (facial disc) and the large eyes are directed to the front rather than to the sides as in most birds. The carriage of the body is usually rather upright. The plumage is curiously fluffy or soft and the flight comparatively noiseless. As may be expected in birds largely of nocturnal habits, bright colours are not evident in the plumage and most owls are clad in a sombre dress of mottled greys and browns.

Tufts of feathers or "ears" often adorn the top of the head and owls are furthermore peculiar in that the eye is shut by the upper eyelid closing down and not by the lower eyelid being raised which latter method is normal among birds. The majority of owls lay their eggs, which are always pure white and almost round, in holes in trees. In the matter of food they are carnivorous.

Owls are found in most parts of the world: the list of Peninsular species is a fairly long one and contains seventeen names, about half of which are recorded from Singapore; only three species however are really common on the island and these are all mentioned in detail below.

[104]

THE FISHING OWL

Ketupa ketupu ketupu (Horsf.)

Malay name:—Burong hantu.

Description:—This is a large pale brown or yellowish-brown bird, in bulk equal to a domestic cock or a pheasant. The upper parts are heavily streaked with black, the lower parts also with long thin black streaks. The wing quills and tail are conspicuously barred with light and dark. The legs are naked, *i.e.* unfeathered, and the bright yellow eyes large and striking in appearance. The sexes are very much alike. This species cannot be confused with any other local species of owl.

Length about 18 inches, wing 12½ to about 13½ inches.

Distribution:—This fine owl is found in Burma and the range then continues down the Malay Peninsula to Java, Sumatra and Borneo. In the Malay Peninsula it is a common bird.

Status in Singapore:—Quite common in the vicinity of Singapore, but a bird of the country-side and coasts rather than of the town areas, but not rarely at dusk one may see their large forms flitting almost silently across the town gardens. We have seen several roosting during the day in quieter parts of the island; they make rather conspicuous objects sitting quite upright on a bough close to its junction with the trunk of the tree.

Field Notes:—The very large owls seen in Singapore are nearly always of this species. We have known one to follow a car along a quiet road for a mile or two.

Other habits:—Ridley notes that he has seen this bird carry off a fruit-bat: the stomach of a specimen dissected by Kelham contained a piece of stick, the jaw-bone of a rat, portions of beetles and dragonflies, some vegetable matter, and lastly a great red centipede measuring 7 inches in length. In Sumatra it is stated to cause much loss to the owners of fish ponds and in that country, according to Mr. E. Jacobson, it usually lays a single egg in the cuplike hollow formed by the leaves of the big arboreal fern *Asplenium*, no nest-material being used. The egg is white.

Another large owl of approximately the same size as the fishing-owl appears to be not rare in Singapore and the neighbourhood but it is certainly not so numerous as *Ketupa*. This is *Huhua sumatrana* which may be suitably called the Malayan eagle-owl. It is a distinctive looking bird with the legs feathered down to the toes and a tuft of feathers growing up from each side of the head. Above it is dark brown with numerous paler bars and below greyish white, plentifully barred with black.

The well-known barn, or white, owl also occurs in Singapore but it is not common.

Drawn by G. A. Levett-Yeats.

THE COLLARED SCOPS OWL.

Otus bakkamoena lempiji.

THE LITTLE COLLARED OWL

Otus bakkamœna lempiji (Horsf.)

Malay name:—Burong hantu.

Description:—This small owl exhibits considerable individual variation in the general colour tone of its plumage, some examples being rather greyer than typical individuals and others much more rufous. Most usually it is dark brown above mottled with pale buff and below pale or yellowish-brown plentifully marked with dark brown spots of irregular shape and finely speckled with a darker colour. The wing quills and tail are banded light and dark. The iris is usually light brown, the bill horn colour washed with green and the feet greyish.

Length from 8 to 8½ inches, wing 5½ to 6 inches.

Distribution:—The collared owl as we know it in Singapore is found in the Malay Peninsula, where it is a common bird, and in Sumatra and Java; but other races of the same species, so nearly allied that they are only to be distinguished by the expert, occur from India to Japan.

Status in Singapore:—This is one of the two common small owls of the island and it would also appear to be more numerous than the brown hawk-owl next to be mentioned. It breeds in Singapore and is found in most localities from the town gardens to the wooded tops of the hills.

Field Notes:—Owls are quite unmistakable when seen on the wing. They are fat birds with very rounded wings and their short neck and large head gives them the appearance when flying of having little or no head at all!

The present species is occasionally seen during the day. Investigation will sometimes reveal one asleep in the most unexpected places. Once, attracted by the excited behaviour of a few sparrows we found one fast asleep in a tall bush just outside the main door of the Raffles Library in spite of the fact that cars had been passing within a few feet of it for several hours. At other times when walking through woods on the island we have seen one, always one only at a time, sitting on a bough high up in a tree resting during the day. But these occasions are accidental and it is not till the dusk has fallen and it is really beginning to get dark that one usually sees this owl. Then he leaves his hiding place, takes a short flight to a neighbouring tree to stretch his wings and sits there in a conspicuous position, looking very foolish and blinking his eyes for a minute or two before settling down to the really serious business of the night. The call note is well-known locally, and indeed one of the common night noises of Singapore, although perhaps not generally recognised as belonging to an owl. Recognition of this note is complicated by the fact that the call of at least one, and perhaps two, other small owls are heard in Singapore, and it is difficult to describe the differences. The present species has a note of two syllables very aptly written by Hume as *"woo-oo"* but the two syllables are frequently not so distinct as this indicates and the voice of the owl seems to us somewhat as follows—*"woeho"*— repeated a varying number of times. The brown-hawk owl's call is more of a "cat-call", a more cheerful, lively note with less of a "whooping" character about it.

Other habits:—The collared owl is a resident bird and of course nocturnal. The food consists chiefly of insects, but no doubt other small living things are eaten.

The eggs are white and almost round and usually laid in a hollow tree, there being little attempt at nest making. Ridley records that this bird sometimes nests on a beam in the roof of a house.

W. E. Maxwell writing to Kelham said: "The punggok, a small owl, has a soft plaintive note, and is supposed to make love to the moon. 'Seperti punggok merindu bulan' ('just as the punggok sighs for the moon') is a common expression in Perak, applied to a desponding lover."

Kelham who had a knack of creating atmosphere when writing of birds, very aptly said: "Round Tanglin, Singapore, on a still evening, their mournful monotonous hoot was commonly to be heard, and soft and low as it seemed to be it was wonderful at what a distance it could be heard, certainly at from a quarter to half a mile".

Another small owl, *Otus malayana*, very like the species under discussion but much greyer in the general tone of the plumage is sometimes found in Singapore. We have seen a specimen captured on Fort Canning but know little of its local status.

[The little collared owl lies up in the daytime well concealed on a leafy branch of a tree or thick high bush and at dusk begins to move about uttering its plaintive little monotonous hoot and catching and eating large flying beetles on which it is said principally to feed. It is said to catch bats; that it can and would eat small birds if it could catch them the writer can vouch for as when he was away from home a well-meaning friend placed one of these owls in the writer's aviary which at that time contained some ten finches and a big cockatoo : the latter, a very self-satisfied owl and some tufts of feathers alone greeted the writer's return!—J. A. S. B.].

THE BROWN-HAWK OWL

Ninox scutulata malaccensis (Eyton)

Malay name.—Burong hantu.

Description:—Entirely dark brown above and unlike the the last species, uniform in colour and not heavily marked or mottled on the upper surface. The tail is banded alternately light and dark and the head is slightly greyer and less brownish than the rest of the upper parts. The underparts are whitish, but so heavily spotted with large rufous brown spots that sometimes, particularly on the breast, the white ground-colour is obscured.

The eyes are bright yellow, the beak almost black and the feet dull yellow.

Length about 11 inches, wing usually just over 7 inches in length.

Distribution:—This and very closely allied forms of the same species not only occur in all the Malaysian islands but throughout India and the Malay Peninsula. Some of the birds that visit the Peninsula, differ in recognisable detail from the birds which breed with us in being slightly larger and darker in colour. These strangers breed in China, Japan, etc. and come south in the winter.

Status in Singapore:—A common bird of which one may from time to time obtain excellent views in the Botanic Gardens and elsewhere in Singapore. It is less numerous than the collared owl, but like that bird it breeds on the island.

Field Notes:—There is little to add to the notes included under this heading in the case of the last species. The bird is met with under exactly the same conditions as the collared owl but as we have already noticed its voice is quite different.

Other habits:—The food consists chiefly of insects and the bird may be seen sitting on a bough or stump in the gloaming and occasionally pouncing down on the ground for a beetle and then returning, flycatcher-like, to its original perch.

THE PARROT TRIBE

(Psittaciformes)

THE Order of Parrots, of which most readers will be surprised to hear that well over 500 species are known, seems to be related to the hawks and owls. Although found in many parts of the world parrots are most numerous in the tropics. They are usually met with in flocks and their food consists largely of fruits and seeds. Many species are most brilliantly coloured and on this account as well as the marked ability of a few to imitate the human voice they are very favourite cage birds. Large numbers are yearly imported into Singapore from Celebes, the Moluccas and Australia and dozens of highly coloured birds of a good many different species may usually be seen in the bird-shops of the town. The parrot tribe may be conveniently divided into two families : the first includes the true parrots with a fleshy tongue while the second family contains the lories or brush-tongued parrots. All our Malayan species, numbering only five of which but three are known from Singapore, belong to the division of true parrots but many of the gaudy imported cage birds to be seen in the Rochore Road shops are lories.

All parrots lay white eggs. When the young bird is newly hatched it is quite naked but later acquires a covering of thick down feathers.

The large white, sulphur-crested cockatoos which are at times seen on the outskirts of Singapore particularly in the tall clumps of trees at Sepoy Lines are birds escaped from captivity.

THE MALAYAN LONG-TAILED PARROQUET

Palæornis longicauda (Bodd.)

Malay name :—Bayan.

Description :—This beautiful parroquet is quite unmistakable and resembles no other local species. It is a typical parrot in appearance except for the tail which in adult birds has the centre feathers very long and almost whip-like. The general appearance presented is that of a grass-green bird with a rose-pink head.

The sexes vary slightly in plumage. In the adult male the crown is bright green, the back pale green, washed with pale blue on the rump, the wings golden green, the quills washed with bluish-green. The underparts are yellowish-green and the tail blue. The sides of the head and the neck are rose-pink and there is a long, broad black "moustachial patch". The female is a very poor edition of the male, the black moustache being replaced by green and the rose colour restricted to small patches on the sides of the head.

The irides are yellow, the beak mostly red and the feet greyish.

Length from 16 to 17 inches; wing about 7 inches.

Status in Singapore :—A common bird but almost exclusively seen as a migrant : it appears in flocks in the late summer and autumn. These may often be seen flying high over the open spaces on the island such as the golf-courses. When the birds settle it is usually on the tops of tall trees.

Distribution :—This is a truly Malaysian bird being found in the Malay Peninsula, Borneo and Sumatra.

Field Notes :—In Singapore one's attention is usually first attracted to this bird by hearing sharp, unfamiliar cries overhead and then glancing up one sees the flock of perhaps a dozen or twenty birds or even more, hurrying along. The birds fly fast and well and their rounded heads and long thin tails streaming out behind reveal their identity. Sometimes they may be seen, usually several together, climbing about in the top of a fruit tree.

[112]

Drawn by G. A. Levett-Yeats.

THE MALAYAN LONG-TAILED PARROQUET.

Palæornis longicauda.

Other habits:—Flocks of these birds will often come down to trees bearing fruit and we have not rarely seen them in the Botanic Gardens from whence Ridley has recorded that the species evidently prefers dry seeds to juicy fruits, being especially fond of those of the Mahang-trees (*Macaranga*) and the "Pagar Anak" (*Ixonanthes*).

In Sumatra they are said by Mr. E. Jacobson to cause much damage by eating the young shoots and leaves of the coconut palms. The same writer states that: "The bill of captured birds is usually covered by a brownish substance, being the dried up sap of the fruits they feed on".

[This bird breeds in holes in trees and lays about four white eggs. It feeds on fruit, berries and, it is said, seeds and grain. It does well in an aviary and will eat bananas in amazing quantity.

Parrots are clean feeders and it is not, perhaps, generally known that they are excellent to eat.—J. A. S. B.].

Two other species of parrots have been recorded from Singapore, but neither of them are common and the species described above is the only member of the *Psittaciformes* we have ever seen on the island.

The others are the blue-rumped parroquet (*Psittinus incertus malaccensis*) and the blue-crowned hanging parroquet (*Loriculus galgulus*). Both are very distinctive looking birds and on account of their short tails not to be confused with *Palæornis longicauda*. *P. i. malaccensis* has the head and rump pale blue, the back blackish, the wings mostly green and the underparts pale greyish-green washed with blue here and there. The female is generally duller and has the blue of the head replaced by brown: wing about 4½ inches.

Loriculus galgulus is very small—about sparrow size in fact. The male is bright grass green with an orange-yellow patch on the back of the neck, a blue spot on the top of the head and a bright vermillion patch on the throat. The rump and upper tail-coverts are also bright red. The female has no red on the throat. The "serindit" is imported into Singapore in large numbers for it is a favourite cage bird with the Malays.

THE PICARIAN BIRDS

(*Coraciiformes*)

THIS Order contains a truly mixed assemblage for here the ornithologist places the kingfishers, rollers, bee-eaters, hoopoes, hornbills, night-jars, swifts and humming-birds. The official guide to the gallery of birds in the British Museum says of the picarian birds: "They differ greatly from one another in outward form, structure and habits, possessing hardly a single feature in common by which they can be distinguished from other allied orders".

The reader, perhaps a tyro commencing to take an interest in birds for the first time, will naturally ask why they are included together in one Order, but perhaps fortunately for us, our space is too limited to allow of this point being discussed at length! Be this as it may our arrival at the unwieldy "Order" of picarian birds breaks up our routine for we cannot generalise on such an assorted collection in the manner which we have hitherto followed and must therefore devote our "chapter" headings from this point onwards to the smaller divisions or "families" of the *Coraciiformes*.

KINGFISHERS

(*Alcedinidæ*)

THE family of kingfishers consisting of a large number of species includes some of the most beautiful of birds. They occur in most parts of the world but in Malaysia and thence east to New Guinea they are particularly abundant. Kingfishers are, almost without exception, birds of brilliant plumage and normally they have a raucous voice and are of unsociable habits. All the species lay round eggs which are glossy white and deposited in a hole in a bank or tree. Naturalists usually divide the *Alcedinidæ* into two sub-families both of which are represented in Singapore. The first of these may be known popularly as the water-kingfishers which may be characterized by the long slender bill which has a keel along the upper mandible. The second sub-family consists of the wood-kingfishers, birds with a stronger, wider bill. The wood-kingfishers which feed largely on insects, small reptiles, etc. are also well represented in Malaya.

Young kingfishers are very queer-looking little beasts. When just hatched they are naked and they never grow any "down" but the adult feathers appear at once, each feather enclosed in a thin tube or sheath. Until the sheaths burst and reveal the feathers the chick suggests a hedgehog in appearance!

Sixteen species occur in the Malay Peninsula. Some of these show a marked preference for certain haunts. Thus the little yellow birds of the genus *Ceyx* like the forest streams but other kinds are rarely found away from salt water: some are true denizens of the jungle and do not feed on fish.

Of the eleven species recorded from Singapore only six are at all likely to be met with, but one or two of these are among the most familiar birds of the island.

The student of birds always recalls that the late Dr. Bowdler Sharpe, the greatest ornithologist who ever lived, published his magnificent monograph of the kingfishers when little more than a boy.

[115]

[The kingfisher in Great Britain is so intimately associated with streams and lakes that one is at first perhaps rather surprised to find in Singapore that some of the very handsome and big forms seem to be just as content away from water as in its vicinity; and in the case of the two species figured in this book this fact is very noticeable: indeed: "kinghunters" is a name often applied to this group of the Family.

The common Indian kingfisher (*Alcedo bengalensis*) which, though rather smaller than, is almost a replica of the English bird, may be seen any day in Singapore on the coasts, in the creeks or even in gardens usually perched motionless on a branch or flying straight like a huge topaz to another coign of vantage: it feeds chiefly on small fish and breeds in holes in banks: it is known as "Rajah udang Kechil".

The white-collared kingfisher and the Malayan white-breasted kingfisher are typical kinghunters and both are abundant in Singapore Island and have rather similar habits. Both frequent the shore as well as compounds quite away from water, though the latter is perhaps less of a marine species than the former: both are very noisy with harsh loud crackling notes though the white-breasted bird makes the most clatter: they are both bold large birds, with very handsome plumage in which blues and greens chiefly catch the eye but can very easily be distinguished by the fact that the former has a black bill and greenish grey legs and the latter a red bill and red legs.

All kingfishers lay several white eggs and usually nest in holes in banks or trees: both the species figured are no exception to the rule. Fish (though neither of the two are divers like the common Indian kingfisher), crabs, lizards, water-insects, spiders, and it is said even butterflies and mice form their dietary.—J. A. S. B.].

THE SINGAPORE STORK-BILLED KINGFISHER

Ramphalcyon capensis hydrophila (Oberholser)

Malay name:—Raja udang; Pĕkaka.

Description:—As in the other local kingfishers the male and female of this bird are very similar in appearance and furthermore the young birds differ from the adults in detail only. Both sexes have the head, neck and entire underparts light brownish-yellow the top of the head being washed with grey or putty colour. The wings, back and tail are greenish-blue, the rump being particularly bright in colour. To our mind the most conspicuous feature of the bird is the deep red beak and the bright red feet. The iris is brown, but the fleshly edges of the eyelids are red.

This is by far the largest of the local kingfishers and adult birds measure about 14 or 15 inches. The wing is about 6 inches.

Distribution:—The stork-billed kingfishers of this genus are found only in the Oriental region. They range from India and Ceylon through Burma, the Malay Peninsula and thence to Java, Sumatra, Borneo, Celebes and the Philippines. The Malaysian birds have been sub-divided into many races and by one authority the form found in Singapore is considered to enjoy but a limited range, viz.:—"Islands of Singapore, Lingga and Bintang, off the southern end of the Malay Peninsula", but we may reasonably infer that it also extends to other islands of the Rhio-Archipelago. The differences between *hydrophila* and the stork-bills of the mainland of the Peninsula are however very slight. The species is a common bird in many parts of the Malay Peninsula and the outlying islands.

Status in Singapore:—This large kingfisher is a shy bird rarely, if ever, approaching the environs of the town but it is often seen on the northern and western coasts of Singapore and is fairly common on the neighbouring islets. It is, with us, essentially a maritime species and is especially fond of the mouths of the large creeks. We have noted it not rarely in the Straits of Johore near Kuala Kranji, Seletar, Punggol, Serangoon and also at Changi. Occasionally it may be seen along the banks of the reservoirs.

Field Notes : —In their essential actions all the local species of kingfishers show a remarkable similarity. They are solitary birds usually seen alone and never under any circumstances in flocks. From a point of vantage, usually a top or outer branch of a tree or a stump sticking out of the water, or a solitary bamboo or stem overhanging the water, they survey the surrounding country. For a long time they will sit huddled up, almost motionless, with their short necks drawn back on their shoulders and thus present the appearance of a sleeping bird. In reality they are very wide awake and the unsuspecting fish betraying its presence by a ripple near the surface of the water or the grass-hopper by releasing a bent blade of grass is instantly spotted: the bird leaves its station, there is a flash of colour, a "plop" in the water and the bird is back again on the perch beating its prey to death against the bough on which it sits, with vigorous shakes of its head. The tapping noise caused by the grass-hopper or fish being beaten and bruised can be heard for some distance and then when the kingfisher is satisfied it throws back its head and the now lifeless prey disappears down the bird's throat—head first. The best way to see the stork-bill is to employ a sampan and explore the lower reaches of those Singapore waterways that empty into the Johore Straits. Then as one drifts along the edge of the mangrove one may see, perhaps a hundred yards ahead, a large highly coloured bird leave its post and plunge into the water causing a fair splash in so doing. When it returns to its seat in the mangrove it may be possible to push the boat closer for a nearer view but usually, on the first sign of danger, the wary bird darts off with a swift, straight flight at no great height over the water and thus it will precede the sampan for perhaps a mile or two always darting away when one is a hundred yards or so distant.

Other habits : —This kingfisher appears to be less vociferous than the other and smaller species found in Singapore. Its food consists, in the main, of fish, frogs and crabs.

[118]

THE COMMON KINGFISHER

Alcedo atthis bengalensis (Gm.)

Malay name:—Raja udang.

Description:—To any reader interested in birds this species must be well-known, for not only is it common in Singapore but in appearance it is almost identical with the kingfisher of the British Isles. Only the specialist recognises the technical differences whereby it is separated from its European cousin.

The ground colour of the upper parts is metallic greenish-blue with bars on the crown and spots on the wings of a brighter or more vivid green colour. The underparts are perhaps best described in popular parlance as reddish-brown or deep tawny or chestnut. On the head the arrangement of the colours is rather complicated and there are broad stripes of chestnut and green. The chin and throat are white and there are large white spots on the sides of the neck.

The iris is brown and the bill black although the greater part of the lower mandible is sometimes red. The feet are bright red.

The total length runs to about 7 inches and that of the wing between $2\frac{3}{4}$ and 3 inches.

Distribution:—As hinted at above this kingfisher is at the most only a local race, an eastern representative in fact, of the common kingfisher of Europe and as such its range may be given as the British Isles and then quite across Asia to Japan in the east and then south throughout China, India, Malaya and east to the Moluccas. *A. bengalensis* is slightly smaller than the European bird but the two forms appear to pass into each other. We have here a good case to illustrate a commonly observed phenomenon in the bird world, viz. that of a species in which the southern or tropical forms are smaller than those found in more Northern or temperate latitudes.

This is a common bird in the Malay Peninsula.

Status in Singapore:—Common on the island, especially numerous along the sea-coasts, rivers, and creeks but also frequently met with in the inland districts wherever there is water. It can often be seen near the lake in the Botanic Gardens.

Field Notes:—Walk quietly round the less frequented side of the lake in the Botanic Gardens every evening for a week and you will be very unlucky if you do not meet with one of these kingfishers!

At one place there are some bamboos overhanging the water and a kingfisher can often be seen sitting on these. If it is intent on watching the surface of the lake it is possible to approach to within a few yards of the bird. When disturbed it flashes away very low down over the water to a bush on the opposite bank. One glimpses bright blue and rufous and perhaps hears a shrill piping call.

Other habits:—With head bent down this bird sometimes hovers over the water, eagerly watching for fish. Its food consists, at least very largely, of small fish. The nest is placed at the end of a tunnel made in a bank near the water but we have not yet seen a nest in Singapore.

Very similar to the common kingfisher in appearance is the Malayan kingfisher (*Alcedo meninting*) but this is not common enough in Singapore to merit more than a short notice. In size it is even smaller than the common species (total length about 6 inches, wing 2½ inches). The colour is again very like that of *A. i. bengalensis* and it may in fact be regarded as a small and very deeply coloured edition of that bird. The upper parts instead of being merely greenish-blue are of the deepest and brightest blue imaginable and on the underparts the bird is quite rufous.

This very handsome little bird may sometimes be seen near the lake in the Botanic Gardens but it appears to be much scarcer than the previous species from which, in the field, it can only be distinguished by a very sharp eye.

Drawn by G. A. Levett-Yeats.

THE WHITE-BREASTED KINGFISHER.

Halcyon smyrnensis.

THE WHITE-BREASTED KINGFISHER

Halcyon smyrnensis fusca (Bodd.)

Malay name: —Raja udang.

Description: —This kingfisher is very much larger than the common kingfisher but considerably smaller than the stork-bill.

The head, neck and abdomen are chestnut, or chocolate brown and the chin, throat and breast being pure white, a very pretty effect is produced, the bird appearing to wear a clean apron! The wings and tail are bright blue with greenish reflections and there is a large black patch on the upper wing-coverts. Iris brown; legs and bill red.

The length is about 11 inches with a wing of approximately $4\frac{1}{2}$ inches.

Distribution: —The white-breasted kingfisher is found in Asia minor and Palestine, thence east through Persia and India to the Indo-Chinese countries as far east as Formosa and in the Malay Peninsula. Curiously enough it is not known from Borneo, Sumatra and Java.

In the Malay Peninsula it is common.

Status in Singapore: —A familiar and common species showing a decided preference for the gardens and woodlands rather than the vicinity of the sea. It is often seen in the Tanglin district.

Field Notes: —This bird resembles the next species to be described, the white-collared kingfisher, in that it is one of the most conspicuous birds of the gardens in the environs of the city. Both are very noisy birds and their continual squawking is one of the most noticeable bird sounds in the Botanic Gardens. Usually seen alone they sit about on the top branches of trees, and remain silhouetted against the sky as they scan the ground for grasshoppers and other small living things on which they prey. The notes of both species are very much alike but readily separated when heard in close proximity.

The present species is the more brightly coloured of the two birds. Its red beak and chestnut underparts are usually notice-able and the striking white patch on the breast also forms a good field-point. In flight *smyrnensis* shows a white patch near the end of the wing.

Other habits:—A country bird that seems as fond of the woodlands and gardens as the common kingfisher is of the water. As could be expected from this fact the food consists largely of insects and small lizards, etc., but small fish are quite welcome.

Drawn by G. A. Levett-Yeats.

THE MALAYAN WHITE-COLLARED KINGFISHER.

Halcyon chloris humii.

THE WHITE-COLLARED KINGFISHER

Halcyon chloris humei (Sharpe)

Malay name: —Raja udang.

Description: —The white-collared kingfisher is more or less the same-looking bird wherever it occurs and only shades of colour and averages in millimetres can split him up into sub-species. Our plate is drawn from one of the very bright specimens known as *humei*. This kingfisher can be confused with no other local species and it is very easily described.

Underparts entirely white, upper parts greenish-blue, especially blue on the wings. A white collar encircles the neck. The upper mandible is blackish, the lower mandible white, the irides brown, the feet slate colour.

Length almost 9½ inches; wing usually just over 4 inches.

Distribution: —The latest authorative writer on the subject considers that the range of *Halcyon chloris* extends as far north as the Philippine Islands, Siam, India, and Abyssinia, as far west as Abyssinia, south to western India, Java, middle, western and northern Australia, and east to the Fiji Islands, the Solomon Islands, etc.

In the Malay Peninsula it is common but is addicted to the sea-coasts, rarely straying from the vicinity of salt water. It is one of the commonest birds of the coastal islands throughout the region.

Status in Singapore: —Very common, abounding along the sea-coasts but also frequenting our gardens and not rarely can be seen on the trees along the roads in some parts of the island. It breeds in Singapore.

Field Notes: —We have heard this bird characterised as a noisy rascal by several residents in the Tanglin area and have at times agreed with them, but more often we have thought that its voice sounded particularly cheerful and optomistic as it floated in through the open windows of the bedroom in the early morning.

Other habits:—Although this kingfisher is commonly seen in inland districts of Singapore it is much more numerous along the coasts and it is one of the common birds of all the small islands near Singapore.

It appears to live chiefly on crustaceans, insects, small lizards, etc., and examples have been observed hammering the shell dwellings of hermit crabs against stones in order to get at the succulent occupant. In spite of the fact that it is such a common bird comparatively little seems to have been recorded of its nesting habits.

A small Malay boy once brought some young birds to us which he said he had obtained near the Botanic Gardens. They were only a few days old, but we could not ascertain the situation of the nest. Our informant said that the nest was reached by climbing the tallest tree in the neighbourhood, and at considerable personal risk, a statement volunteered no doubt in the hope that the rate of renumeration would depend on the physical (but we suspect in this case mental only) exertion of the bird nester!

Other Kingfishers

Somewhat similar to *H. smyrnensis* in appearance is the black-capped kingfisher, and indeed on the wing the two species are quite difficult to identify although when the birds settle there should be little doubt about the matter. In size there is not much to choose between the two although when it comes down to a question of actual measurements *Halcyon pileata*, as our black-capped bird is called, runs a little larger than *smyrnensis*.

The main differences are that *pileata* has a conspicuous black cap bordered by a white collar which runs all round the neck. The upper parts are also deep violet or blue, quite unlike the greenish-blue of *smyrnensis*. The white apron is also much less well defined in *pileata* but this is a character not very noticeable in the field. If the bird is sitting breast towards the observer it will be noticed that the flanks and abdomen are also not chocolate but rather pale yellowish-brown or rich buff in colour.

[124]

The black-capped kingfisher is not rare in Singapore but on the other hand it is much less frequently met with than the white-breasted kingfisher.

There is yet one other kind of kingfisher in Singapore that, like the stork-bill, prefers the wilder, less frequented parts of the island and rarely if ever penetrates into the populated districts. This is the lilac kingfisher (*Halcyon coromanda minor*), much smaller than the stork-bill and quite different in appearance. Broadly speaking the whole bird is rufous in colour, strongly washed with a violet gloss on the upper parts. Only the rump provides a conspicuous change in the plumage and this is white, tinged here and there with pale blue. The beak and feet are reddish. This bird is about 10 inches or a little more in length and the wing measures from 4 to 4½ inches.

It is not rare in the mangrove regions and is commoner on the islets such as the Ayer Merbau group and Pulau Tekong than on Singapore itself. When it dashes past through the mangrove the white patch on the rump proclaims the bird's identity.

The tiny species of the genus *Ceyx* scarcely deserve a place in this book and in five years we have never met with either of the two species recorded from the island, although there seems to be no real reason why they should not be seen in the quieter spots. Both species (*Ceyx tridactyla* and *C. euerythra*) are small birds, the smallest of the Malayan kingfishers in fact, and bulking much less than a sparrow! They are at once recognised by their bright yellow underparts.

ROLLERS

(Coraciidæ)

THE rollers are distributed throughout most parts of the Old World. They are fairly large birds, nearly of pigeon size, and the plumage is often very brilliant in colour. The popular name is derived from their very curious habit of tumbling about during flight, a character especially well marked in the breeding season. The eggs are white. Two forms are not uncommon in Singapore where in certain localities, in the evening, their curious antics in the air may be watched. We not rarely hear the local species referred to as "blue-jays" by Europeans, not an unnatural mistake to make.

THE EASTERN ROLLER

Eurystomus orientalis (*Linn.*)

Malay name:—Tiong batu.

Description:—This is a largish bird of about pigeon-size and jay-like appearance. The beak is broad and short and the feet small. The appearance is that of a bluish-green bird relieved by bright blue patches. The head is blackish above with an oily green sheen and this on the upper parts passes into dark dull green on the back and rump. The tail is black washed with blue. The chin and throat are bright blue and the remainder of the underparts are greenish-blue. The wings are bluish-green but the wing quills are black with a pale sea-green patch which is very conspicuous in flight.

The iris is dark brown but a pleasing touch of colour is provided by the bill, legs and feet which are bright red.

Length about 12 inches; wing 7½ inches.

Some naturalists declare that there are two forms or sub-species of this bird. They say that *E. o. orientalis* is a resident bird with us and can be distinguished on account of the larger amount of blue on the tail and other minor characters, while *E. o. calonyx* with a blacker tail only visits us in the winter months. The evidence available in the Raffles Museum tends to bear out this distinction, for the Museum series is clearly divisible into two sets of birds and of these the birds answering best to the description of the supposed *calonyx* were obtained in the winter months only, whereas some of those which we regard as *orientalis* were obtained in January, February, March, June, July, September, October and November.

Distribution:—It is difficult to define the range of this bird on account of difficulties already explained in dealing with certain other species. If we accept *calonyx* as a species its range may be said to extend from China and then southwards to the Malay Peninsula and Borneo, etc., in the winter; *E. orientalis* on the other hand being the resident form in India, the Burmese countries and Malaysia. Over and above all this the Australian bird seems to differ in no really important way from *orientalis* and *calonyx* and as *E. australis* comes as far west as Celebes, the range of our roller might reasonably be taken yet further afield.

Status in Singapore : —The eastern roller is a common bird frequenting by choice the patches of jungle and the woodlands rather than the town gardens and more open spots. It often visits the Botanic Gardens and we have noted it as comparatively numerous on Bukit Timah and at Changi.

Field Notes : —This is not a gregarious bird, although several may be found in a small area. It is usually seen sitting in a most conspicuous place on the top of a tree or a projecting bough, its lumpy form showing up against the skyline. The "tiong" also chooses exactly these spots for rest. In the evening several, or a pair, may attract attention by their erratic gamboling in the air.

Other habits : —This is a bird of crepuscular habits : it is mainly insectivorous and very fond of beetles. It is normally a forest dweller and lays its white eggs in holes in trees.

BEE-EATERS

(Meropidæ)

THE bee-eaters are birds of handsome plumage and their graceful, almost swallow-like, forms may be seen in the air as the birds hawk for insects, which comprise their prey, in many parts of the Old World. They are especially numerous in Africa, but four species are found in Malaysia. Three of these are open country birds (two are common in Singapore) but the other, *Nyctiornis amicta*, is a forest species and although common enough in places like the Pahang jungles it is not found in Singapore. In Malaysia as elsewhere the bee-eaters food consists largely of bees and wasps, and as may be expected bee-eaters are reported to be very harmful in districts where bees are kept for profit.

For the purpose of breeding most bee-eaters congregate into colonies in sandy river beds where the white eggs are laid at the end of tunnels which the birds dig in the banks much in the manner of sand-martins.

In form they are slender birds with long, curved and pointed beaks, tiny feet and very efficient wings.

THE CHESTNUT-BACKED BEE-EATER

Merops viridis (*Linn.*)

Malay name:—Běberek, Běrek-běrek.

Description:—Two species of bee-eaters are met with more or less commonly in Singapore. As regards general form the plate of *Merops viridis* which we publish will do for both as the chief difference is in the plumage. The sexes are a little different.

In the present species the male has the head, upper neck and back deep chestnut, the rump very pale blue and the tail greenish. The wings are grass green. On the underparts the chin and throat are light blue, the breast and abdomen green, palest on the abdomen; under tail coverts pale blue.

The female differs in lacking the chestnut colour, the head, neck and back being green like the wings.

The iris is red and the bill and feet black.

Length of the male including the long tail feathers about 11 inches; wing about 4½ inches. Without the long tail feathers the length is just over 8 inches.

Distribution:—This bee-eater is found in southern China thence southwards throughout the Malay Peninsula to the Malaysian islands.

Status in Singapore:—A common bird in Singapore said by Ridley to breed in the sand-pits on the Serangoon Road.

We are by no means sure of its movements. At some times it seems to be numerous and others entirely absent, a condition suggestive of partly migratory habits. It is greatly outnumbered in the autumn months by another species which we describe below.

Field Notes:—This bird should need but a very brief introduction to the resident of Singapore because of its conspicuous habits. It is almost the size of a starling but with a long thin tail and is usually seen either flying about in flocks—sometimes at quite a good height in the air or resting,

THE CHESTNUT-BACKED BEE-EATER.

Merops viridis.

usually two or three or even more side by side, on a telegraph wire or branch. When in the air the triangular wings and the noisy note (which to our mind always seems like a distance note of a referees' whistle or the shorter notes of a water whistle) characterise the species.

Other habits:—Bee-eaters are gregarious birds and at times congregate into flocks numbering one hundred or so individuals. Their movements in the air are not unlike those of the swifts and swallows, in the company of which they sometimes hunt. "When burning scrub, the birds often came to catch the grasshoppers driven out by the fire, and at the first puff of smoke, they would hasten to take up their position on the nearest small tree and commence dashing into the smoke after their prey."—(Ridley).

The blue-tailed bee-eater (*Merops superciliosus javanicus*) has the sexes very similar in appearance. The upper parts are mostly green, but distinctly bluish on the rump and tail. A broad black streak passes through the eye. The chin is yellow, the throat rufous and the breast and abdomen green passing into blue on the under tail coverts. It is a slightly larger bird than *M. viridis*, but there is little in it and the wing of *javanicus* only just exceeds 5 inches, so that in the field the two species look very much of the same size.

It is quite a common bird in Singapore but not resident and only seen during the "wet" season. Most of the locally collected bee-eaters in the Raffles Museum are of this species.

Kelham records: "Arriving in great numbers toward the end of September" and we can vouch for their abundance in or near Singapore from November to at least the middle of March. Mr. Wait says that in Ceylon they arrive about the end of August and leave in April. Bee-eaters would be pleasant (and useful) birds to study in Singapore. The species are easy of recognition and daily kept records would perhaps explain the rather curious movements of *viridis* and further-more fix the exact Singapore "season" of *javanicus*.

It may be mentioned here that *M. viridis* is the bird much better known as *M. sumatranus* and is the *badius* of Kelham's paper. *M. s. javanicus* was formerly known as *M. philippinus*. Bee-eaters are almost the only land birds of which we have had direct personal evidence of migration in Singapore where all migratory phenomena are difficult to observe. On certain nights in July we have at times heard large flocks passing over the Gardens. The air would be noisy with their well-known notes and on one evening in particular an enormous number of birds must have passed.

[The chestnut-backed Bee-eater may be seen sitting on posts, exposed branches or very often on telegraph wires looking out for insects which when sighted it quickly pursues and catches. Sometimes when a hatch of some moth or fly brings a swarm of such creatures into the air large parties of Bee-eaters may be seen, in company with other birds, performing graceful evolutions after their prey. Towards evening flocks—sometimes small and sometimes very big—gather together and, after circling about, apparently aimlessly, for a time, settle down to roost in some tall favorite trees which constitute a regular nightly rendezvous: in the Botanic Gardens is such a haunt.—J. A. S. B.].

HORNBILLS

(*Bucerotidæ*)

THE curious-looking hornbills (Malay, Burong Enggang) are not only found in the Oriental region, in many parts of which they are very familiar birds, but members of the family are also found in Africa and the Australian region.

In Malaya no less than eleven species are found, some rare and denizens of the deep jungle, others common and conspicuous inhabitants of the trees near human habitations.

Hornbills have always excited attention on the part of naturalists for not only is their appearance extremely grotesque, but their nesting habits are very strange. The name hornbill is of course derived from the large casque which, varying greatly in shape in the different species, is situated on the upper mandible. One gets the impression that the bird must find its bill rather cumbersome, but this is no doubt not so, for with one exception the bill is not solid but filled with a cellular tissue. Hornbills are furthermore remarkable in that their bones have much larger air spaces than those of most birds and they are also provided with stout eyelashes, rather an unusual feature in birds. They are not skilful in the air although capable of travelling long distances, and the noise made in flying can be heard from afar. This latter fact is no doubt due to yet one other peculiar feature in their construction, the noise being produced by the rush of air through the open bases of the wing-quills which are not covered by the small feathers lining the base of the wing as is usually the case.

The nesting habits of the hornbills are very extraordinary for the female is imprisoned in the hollow tree in which she has laid her eggs, the hole of the nesting cavity being closed up with a clay-like substance. Through a small opening in this manufactured barrier the male feeds his mate. This method seems rather harsh, but perhaps secures immunity for the sitting bird from monkeys and small arboreal carnivorous animals. Much more could be related of the very strange behaviour of hornbills. It could be told how the imprisoned females of some species actually moult their quills during their confinement and grow others and also of how each meal brought by the male for his mate is enclosed in a tough membranous bag.

Some of the details concerning the domestic life of the hornbills are so queer that it is quite easy to understand how it was that the early observers had considerable difficulty in getting stay-at-home naturalists to believe their narratives!

The food consists in the main of berries and fruit but small living animals are also taken.

Three species of hornbill have been recorded from Singapore, the rhinoceros hornbill (*Buceros rhinoceros*), the solid-casqued hornbill (*Rhinoplax vigil*), and a smaller black and white species (*Anthracoceros convexus*), about the size of a raven.

It is difficult to decide as to how much reliance can be placed on the records of the first two species for there is little country in Singapore suited to their requirements: but although we ourselves have not yet seen even the third species on the island there is no reason why it should not be found here, for it is less of a forest dweller than the others and is common not only in Johore, just across the narrow strait of water, but also in the Dutch Islands to the south.

SWIFTS

(*Cypselidæ*)

THE swifts, usually small birds, are so named because of their remarkable powers of flight. The large spine-tailed swifts, examples of which occur in Malaya, include the swiftest of all known birds. In the air swifts are easily confounded with swallows by the uninitiated, but the resemblance in shape and in the method of hunting is no criterion as to the relationship of the two groups which are genetically remote. Swifts are found in most parts of the world. They are essentially aerial in their habits their food consisting entirely of insects captured on the wing.

The feet are extremely small, the mouth very capacious and the wings long and slender.

In the Malay Peninsula some fifteen species are found. These include several tiny species of the genus *Collocalia*, the members of which make the nests esteemed by Chinese for the purpose of making soup.

THE MALAYAN HOUSE-SWIFT

Apus affinis subfurcatus (Blyth)

Malay name : —Layang layang.

Description : —Our plate of this bird almost suffices for a description. It merely is necessary to say that this swift is black with a conspicuous white rump or "tail-patch" and a dirty white throat. There is little difference between the sexes. The irides are brown, the bill and feet blackish.

Length approximately 5½ inches; wing 5 to 5½ inches.

Description : —The Malayan house-swift is a common bird in the Malay Peninsula, Borneo, Sumatra and Java. It extends through Siam into China. In the greater part of India it is replaced by a slighter paler bird, obviously but a race of the same species and there is again another sub-species which was described from Palestine and is found in N. W. Africa and also Kashmir.

Status in Singapore : —Very numerous in Singapore and easily the commonest swift on the island. It breeds freely in the town and nests exist in convenient places in some of the large buildings in the busiest and noisiest spots of the commercial quarters.

Field Notes : —A small, swiftly flying bird with a shrill voice, roughly about the size of a swallow and in flight appearing all black except for a conspicuous white "stern" can be none other than this species.

Other habits : —This swift is familiar to most people on account of its close association with many houses in Singapore. During the breeding season the birds are most confiding dashing to and from their mud-nests, often situated on the roof of the porch of an occupied house, and paying little attention to cars stopping a few feet below them. In the evening they sometimes congregate into large flocks, often in company with bee-eaters, and indulge in aerial evolutions till nightfall. Sit-

Drawn by G. A. Levett-Yeats.

THE MALAYAN HOUSE-SWIFT.
Apus affinis subfurcatus.

ting birds will often leave their nests in the middle of the night and take a hurried dash round. Several dozens of nests may be found clustered together.

[The Malayan house-swift simply swarms in Singapore and in the evening just about dusk thousands may be seen fluttering about Collyer Quay before they retire to roost and uttering their tremulous squeaking cry which is very unlike the loud prolonged scream of the common European species. It breeds in colonies on rafters under eaves or porticos (many used to attempt to nest under the porch of the old General Post Office in the town) and lays as a rule two white eggs: the nest is made of rubbish such as dried grass, feathers and bits of paper stuck together with mud and mucus from the bird's salivary glands.

The famous birds' nest soup, which is such a gastronomic delicacy amongst the Chinese and which is really very nutritious and palatable, is prepared from the little nests of certain small species of swifts usually known as swiftlets (*Collocalia*) of which several kinds occur in the Peninsula: the trade is of considerable importance running into a value of hundreds of thousands of dollars annually: most come from Borneo and the Dutch Islands: the best nests are white and made practically entirely of salivary excretions and are no bigger than a five-shilling piece: they are found in large numbers in caves which are let out to professional "farmers" who handle the business: they can always be bought in Singapore but are by no means a cheap luxury.—J. A. S. B.].

THE MALAYAN CRESTED SWIFT

Hemiprocne longipennis harterti (Stresem.)

Description:—This tree-swift has the upper parts dark oily green and the underparts pale green, lightening to whitish on the abdomen. Behind the eye is a patch of chestnut colour ("ear-coverts").

The female lacks the chestnut patch but is otherwise very similar to her mate.

Irides brown, bill black, feet dark purplish-flesh.

Length 7 to 8 inches: wing between 6 and 6½ inches.

Distribution:—This tree-swift is found in Tenasserim and thence down the Malay Peninsula to Borneo, Sumatra and Java.

Status in Singapore:—Although we have on odd occasions seen this bird near the town it is usually only to be met with in the country districts where it is numerous. It is common in the small islands and apparently resident.

Field Notes:—This is a larger bird than the house-swift and has especially long wings and a very long slender tail. It is usually met with in small scattered parties but this species is by no means so exclusively aerial in its habits as the house-swift: dashing about after insects high in the air is varied by frequent periods of resting on the topmost branches of a convenient tall tree.

Other habits:—The nesting habits of the swifts of this genus are of peculiar interest. The single egg is laid in a "minute saucer-shaped nest, only about 1½ inches in diameter, of flakes of bark and sometimes a few feathers cemented together, and attached to the side of a horizontal dead twig or branch with saliva. The nest is so small that it is with difficulty seen, and the swift sits on the branch with its body over the nest." Thus writes Blanford of *M. coronata* which is the Indian representative of our bird. When the bird is resting

[138]

on a high branch there thus seems no way of knowing whether she is sitting on a nest or not, and even when she flies off it would need a good glass to detect the small nest well above one.

Several other swifts can be seen more or less commonly in Singapore.

The small Malayan spine-tailed swift (*Chætura leucopygialis*) is not uncommon in the rural districts where it may be seen flying over water, perhaps the sea, in the evening. It is a tiny blackish bird with a greyish-white rump. A much larger species of *Chætura* also visits Singapore but it is erratic in its appearances and we have discovered little about it.

At times also, in the evening chiefly, flocks of small and dark-looking swifts appear in flocks in the sky. These are mostly the "edible-nest swifts" or swiftlets of the genus *Collocalia* of which at least two species occur in Singapore.

Another very similar species is the eastern palm-swift (*Tachornis battassiensis infumata*) which on the wing looks identical with the swiftlets. It makes a tiny cup-like nest which is attached to the underside of a palm leaf. The tiny all-black swifts seen in the town gardens are usually examples of this palm-swift.

The tufted tree-swift (*Hemiprocne comata*) is another fairly common local swift. It has habits very like those of *H. l. harterti* and is met with in similar situations, but in Singapore seems rather less common than its larger relative. *H. comata* is a slightly smaller bird, about the size of the house-swift, easily recognised on account of two conspicuous white stripes on the head, one over the eye and another forming a moustache.

NIGHTJARS

(*Caprimulgidæ*)

THE nightjars, or as they are equally well-known, the goat-suckers, are mainly crepuscular or nocturnal in habits. Like the swifts they are well adapted for the aerial life they lead for the legs are very small and weak, the wings long and blade-like and the mouth, which is protected by stiff bristles, very large. The plumage is soft and fluffy like that of the owls. In most cases the eggs are laid on the ground and no attempt is made at nest building.

Nightjars were at one time, and perhaps even now in some country districts at home, regarded with superstition on account of their reputed habit of milking goats. There is of course no element of truth in this belief.

Only four species are found in the Malay Peninsula and of these two are common in Singapore.

The Frogmouths (*Podargidæ*) are nocturnal, picarian birds nearly related to the nightjars towards which they bear a considerable resemblance.

They are only found in the Oriental and Australian regions and three species are known from Malaya. Of these, one has been recorded from Singapore, *Batrachostomus stellatus*, but even supposing this record to be accurate, we very much doubt if the bird will ever be met with again on the island. Here also may be mentioned the well-known Hoopœ Family (*Upupidæ*) which is also found in the Malay Peninsula but not in Singapore.

Drawn by G. A. Levett-Yeats.

THE JAVAN NIGHTJAR.
Caprimulgus macrurus.

THE MALAYAN NIGHTJAR

Caprimulgus macrourus bimaculatus (Peale)

Malay name:—Burong tukang; B. sĕgan.

Description:—Like the owls the nightjars are very difficult birds to describe without resorting to a highly detailed account of their plumage which for our present purpose is most undesirable.

The general effect their plumage produces is that of a highly variegated mass of brown, buff and grey, somewhat like the lichen covered bark of a tree.

In the present species the upper parts are best described as ashy brown with large and irregularly placed and shaped pale buff and black spots and the whole finely mottled with a darker colour. The underparts are buff, narrowly barred with dark brown. There is a large white patch on the throat. The outer tail feathers are also half white and the wing quills have a conspicuous white patch half-way along their length.

The female is very like the male but has no white spots on the wing and tail quills.

Irides, bill and feet brown.

In length this nightjar runs to about 11 inches with a wing of about 7½ inches.

Distribution:—Forms of *Caprimulgus macrourus* are found in India, Burma, Siam, China, the Malay Peninsula and Malaysian Islands and as far east as New Guinea and Australia. The actual form found resident in Singapore has a comparatively limited range including the Malay Peninsula (as far north as Penang) and Sumatra.

Status in Singapore:—This is a common bird on the island but most numerous in the autumn when there is a considerable influx of "foreigners". The local stock thins out very appreciably in spring but some few pairs remain to breed.

Habits:—This nightjar is commoner in cultivated areas than in the dense jungle. It patrols the roads and gardens for its insect food flitting along in a very light manner and sometimes settling on the ground. It does not become active until dusk hiding during the day in bushes in cool shady places. It is usually seen alone although as it is a common species several can sometimes be heard within a short distance of each other.

[It hides during the day and appears as evening falls flying silently to and fro and wheeling round the tops of shrubs and bushes after cockchafers and other insects on which it feeds and which it captures in its capacious mouth. It is often mistaken for an owl. It is common in the Botanical Gardens and indeed all over the Island and when motoring at night one frequently flushes a bird which has been sitting in the sandy road probably enjoying a dust bath and scared by the dazzling head-lights just flits into darkness and safety.

It is best known, however, for its extraordinary cry which sounds like a stone thrown over a pond of ice or a person hitting a hard piece of timber with a stick: this noise is repeated with monotonous regularity—five times, pause, six times pause—ten times, pause and so forth—and on a hot damp night with half a dozen in full cry all round the house, the performance is somewhat tedious and annoying. It is said that the record "break" known is ninety-nine! When engaged in this vocal exercise—it can hardly be called music—the bird stands on a branch; which is clutched by the feet one in front of the other and not side by side as a fowl or sparrow holds to its perch: and if one moves carefully it is then quite easy to get within a few feet of the burong tukan kayu (*i.e.* carpenter bird) as the Malays call it. The note is usually written onoma-topœically "tock-tock-tock".

The nightjars lay two eggs on the ground in a slight hollow: these are so coloured as to assimilate to the surround-ing soil and are difficult to find: two pebbles of equal size being side by side should be looked for.

Nightjars have the inner side of the middle toe nail serrated like a comb: so have pelicans, some of the bitterns and a few owls: the object may be to clean the stiff bristles, which lie about the mouth of the nightjar from bits of scale and debris of insects which impinge on the bird's face as it catches them.—J. A. S. B.].

[142]

THE MALAYAN CRESTED NIGHTJAR

Lyncornis temmincki (Gould)

Malay name:—Burong Taptibau.

Description:—To the casual observer this species looks very much like an ordinary nightjar and indeed making a superficial comparison between the female "tock-tock bird" (we choose the female because of her lack of the conspicuous white spots on tail and wings) and the crested nightjar, the only difference appears to be in the general tone of the plumage, which in *L. temmincki* is rather darker in general effect than is *C. macrourus*.

Closer investigation will reveal the characters that are regarded by systematists as of sufficient importance to place this bird in a separate genus—*Lycornis*. These characters are the absence of the stiff hair-like feathers ("rictal bristles") at the base of the bill and the presence of two small tufts of feathers growing from just above the ear. These tufts are very small and not at all conspicuous.

Like the other nightjars the plumage of this bird is a most complicated affair of dark browns, warm browns, russets and buff and so we must try to strike a broad line of description. The sexes are alike.

The general colour of the upper parts is rich brown, copiously mottled with blackish. The tail and wing quills are dark brown, nearly black in fact, with indistinct bars, *i.e.* broken up bars of rufous or rich brown. On the underparts there is a large white patch on the throat. Following this is dark brown zone in which the feathers have rufous edges. The remainder of the breast, the abdomen and the under-tail coverts are buff with wavy blackish cross-bars. The large eye has the iris brown. The bill is brown and the feet purplish flesh or brownish.

The length is about 10½ inches: the wing 7½ to 8½ inches.

Distribution:—This is a characteristic Malaysian species and is not found outside the area. In the Malay Peninsula it is a common bird.

Field Notes:—To see this nightjar, so very different in general behaviour from the "tock-tock bird", take a car to the Mandai Road, halt against the open ground on the south of the road and wait till the light fails. Then if you are lucky you will hear a pleasant, clear and very distinctly trisyllabic note far away, a long distance above your head. Perhaps glancing upwards you will not be able to locate the bird and the note will sound from another direction and soon perhaps several, even a dozen of these nightjars, will be seen all in sight at once, circling and wheeling in a wonderful manner in the air. They will not come very near to you like *C. macrourus* but from the typical behaviour outlined above there is no mistaking the bird.

Other habits:—Very little has been recorded of the habits of this nightjar. Mr. Jacobson of Sumatra is worth quoting. "Contents of stomach green *Pentatomidæ*, crickets, beetles, flying termites and other insects. These birds leave the forest, where they hide during the day at 6 P.M. exactly. Usually flying very high they follow a valley or seek their feeding places, uttering all the time their call note ("teet-a-bu" or "tap-ti-bau") which can be heard at a great distance.

"Then they descend to a lower level where they can expect a good catch, *e.g.*, above a ricefield, etc. Here they flit to and fro and half an hour later they return to their hiding places, their crops being chockful of insects. Sometimes they return again in the morning at daybreak.

"Their flight is very peculiar and quite different from any other birds I know, very irregular and with many zigzags, from time to time they raise their wings so that they form a right angle and hold them so motionless for some time as they glide through the air.

"Suddenly they interrupt their flight by jerky crochets and turns, making it very difficult to hit them, although the smallest size of shot will bring them down, just like snipe.

"At Balum I observed every evening some thirty birds coming down the valley, they were so regular in the coming and going that I used to set my watch by them. In the time of the Mohamedan fasting the villagers, who possess no watches, know by the arrival of the birds that it is time to break their fast."

[144]

TROGONS

(Trogoniformes)

TROGONS (Malay; burong kasumba) are found in Central and South America, Africa, India, Indo-China and Malaysia but although six species are found in the Peninsula, some being relatively common, America is perhaps to be regarded as the headquarters of the group for there the greatest number of species occurs.

Trogons are birds of the dense jungles. Their plumage is in many cases of extreme brilliancy. Fossil remains of these now tropical birds have been found in France.

The food consists largely of insects which are more often than not captured on the wing. The whitish eggs are laid in holes in rotten stumps or branches of trees.

In disposition trogons are rather sluggish. On account of the extreme delicacy of their skin they are the despair of field collectors. The plumage is very dense and almost owl-like in texture but the skin itself is about as stout as wet tissue paper and we have never yet succeeded in skinning a trogon without splitting the skin somewhere. If one successfully negotiates the rump, then the skin is sure to split when the head is being turned back!

In the Museum it is found that the wonderful orange or pink colours of the males are very fugitive and a few months in a strongly lighted exhibition gallery is quite sufficient to almost bleach a trogon beyond recognition. In fact the only convenient thing about the trogon from the Museum point of view is that the feathers are often numerous enough and sufficiently long to cover up the disastrous work of the heavy-handed taxidermist!

In the Raffles Museum there are recently collected specimens of two species of trogon from Pulau Ubin; these are the Malayan trogon (*Pyrotrogon diardi sumatranus*) and the large Malayan black-headed trogon (*P. kasumba*) but if these are to be found in Singapore now-a-days it is certainly only on very rare occasions and we have never seen an example on the island. Trogons however are so thoroughly characteristic of the region that this book would have seemed incomplete without a passing reference.

[145]

CUCKOOS

(*Cuculiformes*)

MEMBERS of this very large family are found in most parts of the world but they are more numerous in the tropics.

Cuckoos are abundant in this part of the world and in the Malay Peninsula nearly thirty species occur of which some seventeen are recorded from Singapore. While some of these species, like the well-known crow-pheasant, are resident with us many others such as the hawk-cuckoos (*Hierococcyx*) and the koel (*Eudynamis*) are only met with in the winter months.

In appearance tropical cuckoos vary greatly: some are clad in sombre colours, others in metallic greens and violets.

The parasitic habits of some of the species have always directed popular attention to the cuckoos but it should be noted that many kinds are not parasitic but build their own nests and attend to their young in a normal manner.

THE MALAYAN BRAIN-FEVER BIRD.

Cacomantis merulinus.

THE MALAYAN BRAIN-FEVER BIRD

Cacomantis merulinus threnodes (Cab. and Heine)

Description:—In this small cuckoo the adults of both sexes are very much alike in plumage but the young birds are rather different.

In the adult the head, neck, chin, throat and breast are ashy grey, the back and wings are earthy or dull brown, washed with oily green. The tail is black, the feathers tipped with white and varigated throughout their length with white spots and bars. The abdomen and under tail coverts are bright pale brown ("rich buff").

Young birds are quite rufous above and pale buff below, and are almost everywhere marked with dark brown, chiefly in the form of indistinct cross bars. From this barred immature plumage the birds gradually change into the adult dress.

Distribution:—Forms of this small cuckoo are found in Ceylon, India and north to China, thence south through Burma, Siam, the Malay Peninsula and the Malaysian Islands. Even to the east of this, in New Guinea and Australia occur birds which are probably no more than sub-specifically distinct from *threnodes*.

Status in Singapore:—Fairly common in Singapore without being really numerous. It is to be seen in a variety of situations, in the Botanic Gardens as well as in the mangroves.

Field Notes:—This is the small slender bird with the short neck and long tail that sits, all alone, on the very topmost twig of a tree or in a shrub and practises tuneful—but in time very monotonous—scales of several descending notes. To most residents of Singapore its voice is more familiar than its general appearance and one rarely see more of the bird than the small shape, silhouetted against the sky for it flits from one tree top to another.

The English name "brain-fever bird" is almost as suitable as the Malay name which means the deserted child and indeed the mournful little scale reminds one of the constant laments of someone bemoaning his fate.

[147]

This cuckoo is of parasitic habits laying its eggs in the nests of other small birds and leaving the foster parents to hatch and rear the young.

The bird breeds in Singapore but the only nestling we have seen was taken from the nest of the common Iora.

The eggs of the Ceylon brain-fever bird have been found in the nests of tailor-birds.

If the proportion of the sexes shown by a series of locally collected birds is any real indication of the matter it would seem that in this species the males greatly outnumber the females.

THE KOEL

Eudynamis scolopacea malayana (Cab. and Heine)

Description:—The adult male of this large cuckoo is soon described for it is entirely glossy black or, let us say, black with a bluish-green gloss. Admirable touches of colour are provided by the soft parts for the iris is bright red, the beak dull green and the feet grey.

The female is quite a different bird. On the upper parts she is dark brown with a slight greenish gloss and below dirty white or very pale buff. Her most distinctive character is the presence of numerous white spots scattered over the whole of the upper parts and narrow brown bars on the underparts. The tail is banded dark brown and white.

Length about 16 inches; wing 8 inches.

Distribution:—Races of this species occur through India and up to China and then south through the Peninsula and east to Flores. Other members of the genus occur in the Philippines, Celebes and Australia, etc.

Status in Singapore:—This is not a resident bird in Singapore and it would appear that its stay on the island is usually limited in duration, but when it does appear among us as a migrant we have always found it very conspicuous. It turns up in all sorts of places, including the gardens in the town and is such a large bird that it usually attracts attention.

Field Notes:—The koel is nearly as large as a pigeon with a much longer tail. The males appear in about equal numbers with the speckled brown and white females.

The voice is very distinctive when once learned and consists of a loud, penetrating double note. The birds are usually seen trying to take cover in some vegetation for they are not fond of the open.

Other habits:—This is another cuckoo of parasitic habits, in Ceylon laying its eggs in the nest of crows. It is almost certain that the bird does not breed in Singapore.

It is a fruit-eater and has a pleasant voice—not a song of course, but clear, arresting call notes from which the onomatopoeic "koel" is derived.

THE COMMON COUCAL, OR CROW-PHEASANT

Centropus sinensis bubutus (Horsf.)

Malay name:—Bubut.

Description:—The adult of this, the largest of our local cuckoos, is soon described for with the exception of the wings which are chestnut the whole bird is black, faintly glossed with violet or green. Shelford tells us the way in which the crow-pheasant got this bicoloured plumage. He writes: "There is an amusing folk-tale concerning this bird and the Argus Pheasant which runs as follows": Once upon a time the Ruai (Argus Pheasant) and the Bubut met together in the jungle and agreed to disguise themselves with tatu marks, as their enemies were over-plentiful and vigilant. The Bubut tatued the Ruai in a very effective way, as the plumage of the bird bears witness to this day, but the Ruai was lazy and could not be bothered to tatu his friend in return; so, crying out that his enemies were approaching, he picked up the vessel containing the tatu-pigment, poured it over the Bubut's head and then hastily decamped: to this base treatment the Bubut owes its peculiar colouring".

The young bubut is largely barred black and rufous and, as in the other two cuckoos treated of in this book, its appearance is quite different from that of the adult bird.

Irides red, bill and feet black.

Length 18 to 19 inches: wing 8 or 9 inches.

Distribution:—Ceylon and India up to South China and down through Burma and Siam to the Malay Peninsula, Borneo, Sumatra and Java. Within this range there is sufficient variation in size to warrant the recognition of several sub-species.

Status in Singapore:—This bird is fairly common in Singapore but it is extremely local in its distribution and is almost exclusively found in open land, covered with low scrub and long grass, particularly if the ground is in any way swampy.

It is very fond of the railway clearings and the big black and rufous bird can often be seen from the windows of the Singapore-Penang mail.

One or two can sometimes be seen in the Economic Gardens in Cluny Road, and on the small islands hereabouts it is more numerous than in Singapore itself.

Field Notes:—The crow-pheasant is usually seen sitting on the top of a bush or tangled mass of scrub on open ground. He is a crafty fellow and of marked sulking and dodging habits, dropping like a stone into the grass at the first sign of danger and then running away on the ground. On the wing, he looks not unlike an English pheasant. Although the bird may not be well-known at sight the voice is perhaps familiar.

From the bush one hears "toop-toop-toop" or the sound from which the Malays have given him his local name "bubut, bubut".

Other habits:—The food consists of insects and other small living things which are hunted to a large extent on the ground.

This bird makes its own nest, a large globe-like mass of twigs, grass, etc., which contains white eggs and is placed in a bush or tree.

WOODPECKERS, BARBETS AND THEIR ALLIES

(*Piciformes*)

THIS large order contains among others an interesting family with which we are not concerned, *viz.* the American toucans. Examples of three families are known in Malaya, but with the honey-guides (*Indicatoridæ*) we are not concerned. They are soberly clad little birds; most of the species are African but one occasionally turns up in the Malay Peninsula where it is, however, very rare. It is scarcely likely to occur in Singapore.

All the members of the Piciformes have anatomical characters in common, although superficially rather different in appearance. The remaining two families, the woodpeckers, and the barbets, are so well represented in the Malayan region that we will deal with them separately.

WOODPECKERS

(*Picidæ*)

THE woodpeckers are a large family of birds found in most temperate and tropical parts of the world, but curiously enough not in Australia, Polynesia or Madagascar.

About thirty species are known from the Malay Peninsula where they are generically known as "bĕlatok".

In their general appearance and in their habits woodpeckers display a somewhat unusual conformity to type; so much so, in fact, that we shall have but little to say of the various species under the heading of "other habits".

The typical woodpeckers may be recognised by their strong chisel-shaped bill, their stiff shafted and wedge-shaped tail and their long worm-like tongue. This tongue, which is rendered sticky by the supply of a fluid from salivary glands, is used for gathering up insects in the process of which it can be protruded for a considerable length.

Normally the foot has four toes and is nicely adapted to the requirements of a climbing bird in that two toes are directed to the front and two to the rear. The usual method of progression is that the woodpecker starts to climb from near the base of a tree trunk quietly working its way up to the top, going round and round the trunk in the process and gaining considerable support from the stiff tail which is pressed fanwise against the bark. In the course of the climb the bird occasionally stops to search in the bark for food and it is then that the tapping noise, such a well-known sound of the woodlands although easily confused with the creaking of a bamboo, is heard as the bird vigorously taps the tree with its bill.

The voice of the woodpeckers is not musical. In most species it is a scream, in some others it is not unlike the distant neigh of a pony and in yet other species a shrill single note is repeated rapidly several times.

The food is mostly composed of ants and other small insects, especially of the wood-boring kinds. In the majority of species the white eggs are laid in a hole in a tree.

In addition to the typical woodpeckers this family includes the well-known wrynecks, none of which however occur in Malaysia; and some tiny little birds known as piculets occuring in the Malay Peninsula but not yet recorded from Singapore.

Seventeen species of woodpeckers are recorded as having occurred on Singapore Island. A few of these we suspect are rarely, if ever, found with us now-a-days; but a number of species, all mentioned in greater detail below are fairly common and at least five kinds are frequently met with. To recognise all of the seventeen recorded species in the field without previous acquaintance with the birds in a museum would be an almost impossible task, but we have optomistically made the following "field key", choosing where possible those characters which are most easily to be noticed in the field: —

1. { "Crow" size (wing more than 8 inches) ... 2
   { Smaller 3

2. { Mostly dark slate in colour—*Mülleripicus pulveru-*
   { *lentus*
   { Conspicuous white underparts—*Thriponax javensis*

3. { A very conspicuous white or pale rump ... 4
   { No conspicuous "rear" patch to be noticed in
   { flight 6

4. {
A large bird, wing about 6 inches—*Chrysocolaptes xanthopygius*
A small bird, chequered black and white ... 5
}

5. {
Throat and breast uniformly dark—*Hemicercus sordidus*
Throat and breast barred black and white—*Miglyptes grammithorax*
}

6. {
Small birds, sparrow size—streaked and spotted black and white 7
Larger birds, brightly coloured 8
}

7. {
Larger, wing about 3½ inches—*Dryobates canicapillus*
Smaller, wing about 2¾ or 3 inches—*Dryobates auritus*
}

8. {
Wings crimson 9
Wings not crimson 11
}

9. {
Underparts nearly black—*Blythipicus rubiginosus*
Underparts barred black and white—*Callolophus malaccensis*
Underparts green 10
}

10. {
Top of head red, throat green—*Picus continentis*
Top of head green, throat black and white—*Chrysophlegma humii*
}

11. {
Bright red rump, golden back 12
Large green birds, no red rump 13
Entirely rich brown with black transverse bars—*Micropternus brachyusus*
Dark with pale transverse bars—*Miglyptes tukki*
}

12. {
3 toes (not exactly a field character!)—*Dinopium javanense*
4 toes—*Chrysocolaptes chersonesus*
}

13. {
Underparts uniform and dark—*Chloropicoides peninsularis*
Underparts conspicuously streaked—*Picus vittatus*
}

[154]

THE BAMBOO GREEN WOODPECKER

Picus vittatus vittatus (Vieill.)

Description:—As in most woodpeckers the sexes of this bird vary slightly but in no great degree.

The male is not unlike the common green woodpecker of Great Britain and is roughly the same size. Generally speaking the bird is grass-green with the underparts plentifully streaked with paler green. The top of the head is bright red and there is a black moustache. The wing quills are barred with white.

The female has the top of the head black instead of green but is otherwise similar to the male.

Length about 10½ inches and the wing 5 inches.

Distribution:—Woodpeckers either identical with the bamboo-woodpecker as found in Singapore, or so closely allied that they are only to be distinguished by the expert, are found in Indo-China, in the Malay Peninsula, Sumatra and Java.

Status in Singapore:—We have seen this bird not rarely in the mangrove areas. The underparts of several specimens collected were sullied with mud, suggesting that the bird had been feeding on the ground or at least on the roots of the mangrove.

This is not a garden bird or one likely to be found near the town.

THE BANDED RED WOODPECKER

Callolophus mineatus malaccensis (Lath.)

Description:—The sexual difference in the plumage of this bird are for the purpose of this book not worth mentioning.

The top of the head and wings are dull crimson, the wing-quills black, spotted with pale brown, back and rump bright green, washed with yellow on the rump. On the underparts, the throat and breast are rufous perhaps spotted with black, but the rest of the underparts are barred with black and white.

The beak is mostly slaty; the irides red and feet greenish.

Total length about 10 inches; wing 5 inches.

Distribution:—This bird is found in Tenasserim, the Malay Peninsula, Borneo and Sumatra. In the Malay Peninsula it is fairly common.

Status in Singapore:—One of the common woodland woodpeckers and sometimes seen in the Botanic Gardens.

THE COMMON GOLDEN-BACKED WOODPECKER

Dinopium javanense javanense (Ljung)

Description:—The male is a most handsome bird with the top of the head and the rump bright red. The back and wings are golden-green, the wing-quills and tail black. The entire underparts are boldly spotted with black and white.

The female is like the male except that she has the red colour of the head replaced by a black cap spotted with white.

The bill is almost black and the legs dull green.

Length about 11 inches, wing 5½ inches.

Distribution:—From India this common woodpecker ranges east through Siam, etc. and is found in Burma, the Malay Peninsula, Sumatra, Java and Borneo. In the Peninsula it is a common bird near the coasts and is particularly fond of coconut ground.

Status in Singapore:—With the possible exception of the tiny *auritus* to be mentioned below, this pretty species seems to be the common woodpecker of Singapore. At the same time we have never observed it near the town or in the Botanic Gardens; but in the rural districts, the patches of jungle and the mangrove especially, it is quite common. On the small islands near Singapore it is particularly numerous.

Other habits:—Mr. H. C. Robinson writes: "This species is eminently a denizen of cultivated lands, and I have hardly ever seen it outside the groves of coconut and Penang palms which surround every Malay village. It feeds mainly on ants, principally the tailor-ant (*Oecophylla smaragdina*), but I have observed it attack and swallow a small flying lizard (*Draco volans*).

[156]

Drawn by G. A. Levett-Yeats.

THE MALAYAN PIGMY WOODPECKER.

Dryobates nanus auritus.

THE MALAYAN RUFOUS WOODPECKER

Micropternus brachyurus squamigularis (Sundev.)

Description:—The differences between the sexes are trivial and both cock and hen are entirely dull rufous, barred on the back, wings and tail and abdomen with black; in fact this bird is quite unlike any other local woodpecker.

The beak and feet are slaty in colour.

The total length about 8 inches; wing 4½ inches.

Distribution:—Local races are common in the Malay Peninsula, Sumatra, Java and Borneo and the bird as a species ranges to the Himalayas and China.

Status in Singapore:—We cannot say much of this woodpecker beyond mentioning that it seems to appear fairly frequently in the gardens. Mr. Ridley, at one time Director of the Botanic Gardens, writes: "But the most interesting of these birds is the curious red *Micropternus brachyurus*. This bird always makes its nest in that of one of the tree-ants. The ants form a large black nest in a tree and the bird, which feeds largely on them, digs out a burrow and puts its own nest therein. It has been stated that these ants do not bite, but this is not the case; though small they are most vicious. The woodpecker nested for some years in a tree (*Mimusops Elengi*), close to my house, but the ants' nest collapsed one year, and the birds finding it gone on their return in the breeding season, went away".

THE MALAYAN PIGMY WOODPECKER

Dryobates nanus auritus (Eyton)

Description:—This is a tiny bird about the size of, or in bulk perhaps even smaller than, a sparrow. With the exception of the male which has a tiny red fleck behind the eye the plumage is entirely black and white. The top of the head is black, the underparts dirty white with dark streaks and the back and wings black with broad white bars.

The iris is greyish or dirty pink, the beak slaty in colour and the feet greyish-green.

Total length about 5 inches, wing approximately 2¾ inches.

Distribution:—Siam and Cochin-China through the Malay Peninsula to Sumatra, Java and Borneo.

Status in Singapore:—This is certainly the most frequently seen of the local woodpeckers. It may sometimes be observed on the trees in the Cathedral grounds, and in the Botanic Gardens it is not uncommon. In the Economic Gardens in Cluny Road we have often seen it climbing the larger trees.

Field Notes:—This is a rather shy little bird which, with its small size and inconspicuous type of coloration, makes it rather difficult of observation. We have usually seen it creeping about the trunk, or the boughs, of large heavily foilaged trees and have noticed it, as often as not, entirely by chance.

From the office at the Raffles Museum we have seen birds in the top-most branches of the larger trees in the compound.

By examining all the large trees in the Economic Gardens with binoculars one would be almost certain to locate one of these woodpeckers.

Other Woodpeckers

The Malayan black woodpecker (*Thriponax javensis javensis*), one of the very largest of local species, is unmistakeable in appearance, the male being black with a white belly and bright red head. We have never seen one in Singapore and the bird cannot be common here; but Mr. Ridley mentions that in the Botanic Gardens a pair once remained for some time in a large Jelutong tree. This bird is not uncommon on the Dutch Islands lying to the south and within sight of Singapore so it may still be expected to visit us occasionally.

The crimson-winged green woodpecker (*Picus puniceus continentis*) is very like the banded red woodpecker in size and general appearance but it has the underparts green and not conspicuously barred as in that species.

[158]

Although it certainly occurs in Singapore we cannot say anything very definite as to its status having only seen an odd bird here and there from time to time.

Yet another green woodpecker with a red crested male is Raffles' Three-toed woodpecker (*Chloropicoides rafflesii peninsularis*). This bird also seems to be not uncommon locally and we have repeatedly observed it on Pulau Ubin. It is possibly more numerous with us than in most parts of the Malay Peninsula.

The Burmese Pigmy woodpecker (*Dryobates canicapillus canicapillus*) is extremely like *D. auritus* in appearance but just a trifle larger. In Singapore it has been confused with this latter species but, although it may from time to time occur here, we are confident that the really common small black and white woodpecker hereabouts is *auritus* and not *canicapillus*. The Malayan bay woodpecker (*Blythipicus rubiginosus*) is a very dark brown almost blackish bird with dark crimson back and wings : it has been recorded from Singapore but we have never seen it on the island.

Three small species, the fulvous-rumped barred woodpecker (*Miglyptes tristis grammithorax*), the buff-necked barred woodpecker (*Miglyptes tukki*) and the grey and buff woodpecker (*Hemicercus concretus sordidus*) are sufficiently described in the key. *Chrysophelgma mentale humii* has the top of the head and back green, a bright yellow crest on the nape, the throat white with bold black spots, the foreneck and breast chestnut, the wings crimson and the remainder of the under-parts green.

The fiery-rumped woodpecker (*Chrysocolaptes validus xanthopygius*) has the top of the head and the underparts bright red, the upper parts very dark brown, except the rump which is of a very lively yellow colour. The wings are banded with rufous. The female is much duller in plumage. These five species are not common locally.

The great slaty woodpecker (*Mülleripicus pulverulentus*) is also said to occur in Singapore but we have never seen one on the island. Tickeel's golden-backed woodpecker (*Chryso-colaptes gutticristatus chersonesus*) is so like the common golden-backed woodpecker (*Dinopium javanense javanense*) that it would take a sharp eye to distinguish the two species in the field : the latter is by far the commoner bird.

BARBETS

(*Capitonidæ*)

BARBETS occur in tropical America and Africa but are particularly characteristic of the Oriental region where a large number of handsome species are found. Most of the Malayan species, about a dozen kinds, are green with the head and neck gorgeously patterned with vivid reds, blues and yellows.

In stature barbets are "stumpy" birds, with a stout business-like bill which has strong black bristles at its base.

They live almost entirely in the trees and are essentially forest birds. In Malaya the food consists of fruit and perhaps insects.

In habits they are rather sluggish but their presence is often betrayed by their noisy notes; in some species, such as *Xantholæma hæmacephala*, of such a metallic character that the bird is well-known to Europeans in India as "the coppersmith" and to the Malays in the north of the Malay Peninsula as *tukang besi* ("blacksmith").

Barbets are by no means common in Singapore but a small brownish species, the brown barbet (*Calorhamphus fuliginosa hayi*) and a larger kind, the Malayan blue-throated barbet (*Chotorhea rafflesi*) are not rare. *C. rafflesi* is of the typical appearance indicated above. We have seen it in trees on the shores of the local reservoirs.

BROADBILLS

(Eurylæmiformes)

THE broadbills, so called from the peculiar shape of their short and pointed, but extremely broad flat bills, have by some naturalists been regarded as a division of that great assemblage of birds grouped together into one great order, the Passiformes, and in truth the broadbills share many important anatomical characters with the perching-birds. They are however more usually kept by themselves in an Order apart and a reasonable view of their systematic position seems to place them between the picarian and perching birds.

They were at one time regarded as being absolutely characteristic of south-eastern Asia and Malaysia but it has recently been suggested that a somewhat aberrant African bird should rightly be regarded as a member of the *Eurylæmiformes*.

Most of the species are brightly coloured and all are squat, fat little birds, fond of the jungle and subsisting, it would appear, chiefly on insects. The large globular nest of grass, etc., contains eggs which are either white or buffy in colour, sometimes spotted at the larger end. In the Malay Peninsula no less than seven species are found and of these all have been recorded from Singapore except two handsome genera, *Psarisomus* and *Serilophus* which are only found on mountains.

Most of the local records were made years ago and with the exceptions noted below broadbills are rarely, if ever, found on the island now-a-days.

THE BLACK-AND-RED BROADBILL

Cymborhynchus macrorhynchus malaccensis (Salvad.)

Description:—This is a very brightly coloured bird and quite unlike any other local species. In general appearance it presents a combination of black and dark red with white streaks on the back. In detail, the top of the head, the back, tail and wings are black although when the bird spreads its tail some white spots can be seen. The scapulars are white, rump and entire underparts, except a band across the throat and the chin, are dark red. The edge of the wing orange.

The soft parts of the bird are rather striking in colour. The beak presents a combination of bright blue and yellow.

The feet are also blue and the irides are green, a most unusual colour for a bird's eyes.

Length about 9 inches, wing 4 inches.

Status in Singapore:—This very conspicuous and quite unmistakable bird is not common in Singapore but is likely to be seen at times by visitors to the less frequented parts of the island. We have never seen it in the Gardens but have met with one or two on several occasions in the country at the end of the Chua Chu Kang Road. It breeds on the island.

Field Notes:—A bold red and black bird about the size of a thrush with a dash of white in its plumage and an amazingly blue porcelain-like bill is the impression created by this "gaper" in the field.

Other habits:—We regard the relative scarcity of this handsome bird in Singapore as due to its destruction by Chinese "sportsmen", who never allow a brightly plumaged bird to escape if only they can get near enough to avoid missing it and therefore wasting a cartridge!

It is quite numerous on Pulau Ubin. Kelham notices the species as being shy, and particularly silent and, except during the breeding season, rather inclined to be solitary. From Sumatra Mr. E. Jacobson writes: "The bird lives in secondary forest, on the edge of clearings and near villages. It is not

THE BLACK AND RED BROADBILL

shy at all for I saw their nests made in the trees of a road,
another at the outskirts of a village overhanging a pond. The
nest is globular with its entrance a hole on one side. If the
bird is sitting on its eggs the blue and yellow bill is seen before
the entrance hole. The nest is attached to a thin twig, sometimes not higher than three metres from the ground".

The eggs are whitish with brownish markings.

This is an insectivorous bird.

Another broadbill is not uncommon on Pulau Ubin. This
is the green broadbill, gaper or tody (*Calyptomena viridis*) a
fat, short-tailed, large-headed little bird, grass-green with
black markings.

Ridley wrote of this species with reference to the Botanic
Gardens: "May at times be seen in the denser wooded spots,
quickly passing from thicket to thicket, and concealing itself
among the green leaves".

PERCHING BIRDS

Passeriformes

THIS great Order is by far the largest division in the bird-world. The trivial name is derived from the fact that the feet have three toes pointing to the front and one to the rear an arrangement admirably suited for perching. The many members of the Order, for the most part small birds, are linked together by certain structural characters the most important of which are probably the arrangement of certain tendons in the foot and the character of the bony palate in the skull.

Many of the most familiar birds belong to the Order including the well-known song-birds, the thrushes, warblers, finches, wagtails, swallows, tits and a host of others. Quite a number of "passeres" are normally ground dwellers rather than arboreal in habits.

The main divisions of the Order have regard to the structure of the organ of voice (syrinx) but the number of birds with which we have to deal is so large that it seems advisable to treat each family separately exactly as we did in the case of that miscellaneous array, the *Coraciiformes*.

Evolutionists consider that the Passeriformes include the most highly developed of all birds. They are, as it were, at the top of the avian tree or, as it can be expressed in another manner, the most remote from the reptile-like ancestors of birds.

PITTAS

Pittidæ

PITTAS, or ant-thrushes as they are sometimes called, are found in Africa and thence throughout the Oriental region as far east as Australia. They are birds of very brilliant plumage, normally found in deep jungles and very difficult of observation on account of their terrestrial habits. They are furthermore of a shy disposition and when disturbed hasten off through the undergrowth with astonishing speed, trusting largely to their legs as a means of escape. They are plump little birds, generally about thrush-size with longish legs and a short tail. The nest is placed on, or near the ground, and the eggs are white with dark spots. Seven species occur in the Malay Peninsula and the Indo-Australian area may perhaps be regarded as the headquarters of the family.

THE LARGER BLUE-WINGED PITTA

Pitta megarhyncha, Schleg

Malay name :—Burong Pachat.

Description :—Broadly speaking this is a thrush-like bird with a short tail, longish legs and very brilliant plumage the general scheme of which is green above, creamy brown below and with a bright red patch under the tail.

Top of the head brown, sides of the head black, chin and throat white. The back green, the rump bright blue and the tail mostly black. The wings have the upper coverts bright blue and the quills black with large white patches. The underparts are very pale brown or very dark creamy colour with the centre of the abdomen and the under tail-coverts bright red.

The irides are brown, the bill black and the feet fleshy colour.

Length about 8 or 9 inches; wing 4½ to 5 inches.

The sexes are similar in colour.

Distribution :—This bird has a limited range compared with most of the birds dealt with in this book: it is only found in Burma, Tenasserim and the Malay Peninsula.

Status in Singapore :—A resident bird in Singapore and found more or less commonly in the mangrove on both sides of the Straits of Johore and also on the small outlying islands. Along the edges of creeks on the northern coast of Singapore it may often be seen.

Field Notes :—Like other pittas this must be looked for on the ground. It comes to the edge of the mangrove to bathe and the brilliant plumage, particularly the green back and bright red under tail-coverts reveal its identity. It is easily alarmed for it is a shy bird and then hastens off with very long hops through the mangrove trees keeping close to the ground and leaping from root to root.

Other habits:—Very little seems to have been recorded about the habits. It is apparently resident wherever found. The food consists of molluscs and insects.

Other Pittas

Three other species of pitta are known from the island, but of these we doubt if the Malayan scarlet pitta (*Pitta coccinea*) will ever occur again within our limits. It is a handsome bird with bright blue upper parts and mostly rich red below. The other two species are very like *P. megarhyncha* already described but one, the lesser blue-winged pitta, *Pitta cyanoptera*, has a broad dark streak down the centre of the brown crown and the other *Pitta cucullata*, has the head and neck all black. Examples of both these species have come to hand of recent years and indeed *P. cyanoptera* is not uncommon at times in Singapore.

It only occurs as a migrant: we have at times seen it in the Botanic Gardens, but cannot improve on Ridley's brief but very accurate sentence, "Like all ant-thrushes it remains concealed in the bushes the whole day, usually hopping about the ground. If the thicket is a small one the bird is easily approached as it will not leave the shade unless absolutely compelled, but just after dark it begins its loud call, and will come up quite close, even from a considerable distance, if it is imitated. During the night it is silent, but commences to call again just before sunrise, ceasing when the sun is up".

SWALLOWS

Hirundinidæ

A brief glance at the general form of a swallow's body is sufficient to indicate that it is essentially a creature of the air and indeed its insect food is captured on the wing.

Swallows, of which a large number of species are known, are found all over the world.

On account of a superficial resemblance they were at one time thought to be related to the swifts, but later research revealed important structural differences between the two groups.

A large number of the species are migratory and their breeding habits show considerable diversity. It will for instance be recalled that the common swallow and the house-martin of England make mud nests which are attached to houses whereas the sand-martin deposits its eggs at the end of a tunnel which it digs in a bank.

Very few species are found in the Malay Peninsula: the most interesting is perhaps *Hirundo badia*, a handsome bird with the underparts entirely bright chestnut. It is restricted in range to the vicinity of limestone hills.

THE JAVAN SWALLOW

Hirundo javanica abbotti (Oberh.)

Malay name:—Layang layang.

Description:—In general appearance this bird is very like the European chimney-swallow.

The upper parts are glossy black with a bluish tinge, the forehead, chin and throat chestnut and the underparts pale ashy colour turning whitish on the abdomen. When the tail is spread it can be seen that the tail quills are decorated with white spots just like a row of buttons.

Total length about 5 inches; wing just over 4 inches.

Distribution:—This swallow is found in India, the Malay Peninsula, throughout the Malaysian Islands and eastwards even as far as New Guinea.

Status in Singapore:—Two distinct species of swallows are found in Singapore. They fraternize and are often found flying in the same flock and indeed sitting side by side on the telephone wires and other favourite perches. One of these is the eastern representative of the well-known European swallow. We may well call it the Eastern swallow (*Hirundo rustica gutteralis*): it is distinguished from the Javan swallow by its much longer tail, whitish underparts, and the presence of a blackish patch between the chestnut throat and white breast. *H. javanica* has a relatively shorter tail and dark brownish grey underparts. Both species have a chestnut throat. The Javan swallow is resident in this part of the world: the white breasted bird is purely migratory, not breeding in Malaya.

Field Notes:—As no other swallow-like birds are met with in Singapore the two species mentioned above should be readily identified.

Other habits:—The Javan swallow has the habits more or less common to the typical swallows. It catches its insect food on the wing and constructs a cup-like mud nest which is usually attached to a human habitation. The eggs are white, spotted with brown and greyish brown.

[169]

FLYCATCHERS

Muscicapidæ

THE flycatchers form a very large family of birds in geographical range restricted to the Old World. More than forty small species are known from the Malay Peninsula but of these some are only migrants appearing on the mountains, or on the islands in the Straits of Malacca, in the winter. Certain local species usually attributed to this family could perhaps be equally well placed with the warblers (*Sylviidæ*) and it seems that the division between the two great groups is by no means well defined. In the flycatchers the bill is usually considerably flattened and at its base are strong bristle-like feathers.

Some species have their habitation in the deepest jungle, others prefer the higher zones on the mountains, some are normally inhabitants of the mangrove belt and others yet again are familiar residents in our bungalow gardens.

The plumage may be of the soberest description imaginable, just a combination of dull grey or brown, but in other species vivid orange contrasts with jet black and tne brightest blue with lively red.

Normally, flycatchers keep to the bushes and trees, not searching for their food on the ground. They usually take up a station on a bough and wait silently until an insect flies by. Then they sally forth and having made their capture return to their favourite look-out post.

THE JAVAN FANTAIL FLYCATCHER.
Rhipidura javanica.

Drawn by G. A. Levett-Yeats.

THE JAVAN FANTAIL FLYCATCHER

Rhipidura javanica (Sparrm.)

Malay name:—Murai gila.

Description:—This flycatcher has the upper parts all very dark brown or sooty black but with a broad white end to most of the tail feathers. The underparts are white except for a broad black band across the chest.

The irides are brown, bill and legs black.

Length about 8 inches, wing usually just over 3 inches.

Young birds have rufous markings on the dark parts of the plumage.

Distribution:—This flycatcher is common throughout the whole of the Malaysian area.

Status in Singapore:—A common garden bird but also found, usually in pairs, in other parts of the island, in the woodlands and mangrove alike. It appears to be especially numerous in the coastal gardens in the vicinity of Beting Kusa and Tanah Merah and also near Changi.

Field Notes:—This active little bird well deserves its Malay name of "murai-gila"—or "mad thrush" purely on account of its erratic actions. In the field it may be identified by its jerky, dancing movements, the shuffling of its wings and the continual jerking and spreading fanwise of its long tail.

Other habits:—The small insects which compose the food of this bird are captured on the wing.

The bird has a pleasing little song.

The nest is extremely well made, a tiny, well knit and compact cup usually placed in a horizontal branch. The only one we have seen was found in mangrove and was cup-shaped. Mr. Stuart Baker writes, "the nest is cone-shaped with a tail pendent below it and may be placed either on a small branch or from a small bamboo-twig in open country, gardens, or compounds".

In addition to the species mentioned above one or two other flycatchers are not uncommon in Singapore. Two dull grey kinds, *Alseonax latirostris* and *Muscitrea grisola* are not rare. The former is only a winter visitor but the latter without doubt breeds locally; young birds have the wing strongly washed with rufous and could be mistaken for a species of *Rhinomyias*—a genus not represented in Singapore.

In the mangrove a member of the genus *Cyornis* (*C. rufigastra*) is not uncommon; it has bright blue upper parts and tawny underparts.

CUCKOO-SHRIKES

Campephagidæ

THE cuckoo-shrikes, not a very extensive family of Old World birds, may perhaps be regarded as a link between the flycatchers and the shrikes. They differ from the shrikes in that the feathers of the rump are rather spiny in character. They are arboreal and insectivorous in habits.

The beak is slightly hooked and the sexes sometimes very different in plumage.

In the Malay Peninsula the gorgeous little minivets are perhaps the most striking members of the family: in some species the males are clad in a livery of black and scarlet whereas the females of the same species are black and bright yellow. As the young males first resemble the females in plumage they present a very vivid appearance when assuming the scarlet adult dress.

THE PIED CUCKOO-SHRIKE

Lalage nigra nigra (*Forst.*)

Description:—The male and female of this bird differ greatly in the colour of the plumage.

The male has the top of the head, back, wings and tail glossy black, but the wings and tail with conspicuous white markings. The rump is pale grey and the underparts dirty white slightly washed with grey.

The female (figured in the plate) has the black upper part of the male replace by brownish grey and the whitish underparts have thin dusky bars.

The iris is brown or dull red and the bill and feet black.

Length about 6½ inches, wing 3½ inches.

Distribution:—This cuckoo-shrike or a closely allied form is found in the Nicobar Islands, the Malay Peninsula, Java, Sumatra, Borneo and the Philippines and even the birds of countries yet further east could no doubt be linked up with the present species.

Status in Singapore:— This is a common bird in Singapore, but like the Malayan nightjar it seems to withdraw in the breeding season and to become particularly numerous in the autumn months. At this latter season young birds predominate.

Kelham definitely states that the bird breeds in Singapore and mentions seeing young birds at Tanglin on 1st September, but he does not say how young the birds were and we should like further evidence of the breeding of the bird on the island. Some birds migrate and are found long distances from their breeding grounds when they are almost incredibly young. In Singapore the species usually appears in very scattered flocks, the birds flying from bush to bush or from pole to pole on the tennis courts after the fashion of shrikes.

THE PIED CUCKOO-SHRIKE.

Lalage nigra.

THE PIED CUCKOO-SHRIKE

Field Notes:—The fully adult male in his striking black and white plumage can be mistaken at a casual glance for the straits-robin, but two or three minutes observation of his restless behaviour and smaller size should decide the point. The young birds and females should give no difficulty.

Other habits:—This is essentially not a bird of the forest land and it is usually seen in the open and round about villages and cultivation.

It feeds on insects and the males at least have a characteristic loud, clear whistle.

All the bright red and black or yellow and black cuckoo-shrikes (*Pericrocotus*) are rare in Singapore, but two species in which the males are all grey and the females barred below are sometimes seen. One of these is small (about the size of *L. nigra*) and may be called the Malayan cuckoo-shrike (*L. fimbriata culminata*).

The other kind is roughly the size of a green-pigeon or sparrow-hawk. It is known as the large cuckoo-shrike, *Coracina sumatrensis*. It almost certainly breeds locally and is not uncommon. It is a very noisy bird and usually found in pairs.

BULBULS

Pycnonotidæ

THE bulbuls, of which nearly forty species occur in the Malay Peninsula, are essentially arboreal in habits. Many of them are songsters of considerable merit. Their powers of flight are not particularly well developed and the feet are weak rather than strong in character.

In Malaya all the species are resident. Some kinds are characteristic of the gardens and open country; others are true inhabitants of virgin jungle.

Bulbuls are not found in the New World. With a few exceptions the plumage is dull and not very striking.

The list of Singapore bulbuls is rather a long one and in addition to the several kinds mentioned in detail below quite a number of others have been recorded from the island. Certain bright green species belong to the genus *Chloropsis* and of these the malachite-shouldered green bulbul (*C. viridis zosterops*) seems to be not uncommon in the mangrove areas. *Iole olivacea* which we may call simply the olive bulbul, is not uncommon but would be very difficult to identity in the field as it is so much like several dull species included in the genus *Pycnonotus*: suffice it to say that it has white irides and that from all other species it can be distinguished by the lanceolate feathers of the crown. The red-whiskered bulbul (*Otocompsa jocosa erythrotis* Bp.) can be seen in some parts of Singapore but has no doubt been introduced through human agency. It may be mentioned that some of the birds which we here include under the *Pycnonotidæ* are by some naturalists counted as members of the next family, a very mixed group of small birds known as the babblers or *Timaliidæ* but the change is comparatively recent and we have here followed the older arrangement.

[176]

THE COMMON IORA

Aegithina tiphia tiphia (*Linn.*)

Description:—The common Iora is a bird of sparrow-size, both sexes of which at a distance of a few yards appear yellowish, the male almost canary-like particularly when one is regarding him, as one usually is, from below. The sexes are rather different in plumage.

In Indian birds in the breeding plumage the male has the upper parts including the wings and tail mostly black with white bars across the wings; the underparts are yellow. In the "winter" or non-breeding plumage much of the black of the upper parts is replaced by green.

The female is yellowish green above and below, the wing quills brown but with yellowish edges. There are white bars across the wings.

The irides are straw colour, the bill slaty blue and black and the feet slaty blue.

Total length 5 to $5\frac{1}{2}$ inches; wing about $2\frac{1}{2}$ inches.

The males found in Borneo and Sumatra do not turn black on the back and head in the breeding season like Indian males and it would appear that birds from the Malay Peninsula are intermediate between the two extremes, occasionally though by no means always, developing the back mantle and head. The males in Singapore are often largely black above.

Distribution:—The common Iora has been divided into several races, the plumages of which are of special interest to the ornithologist. Both sexes of the bird as found in Java are, for instance, very similar to that of the female of the race inhabiting the Malay Peninsula. For the purposes of this book it may be said that the Iora is found in India, the Indo-Chinese countries and Malaysia.

[177]

Status in Singapore:—This is a common bird in gardens and woodlands. It escapes general notice because of its habit of frequenting tall trees rather than the sides of the paths, the bushes and hedges. It nests in the town gardens.

Field Notes:—By walking along the paths of the Botanic Gardens and gazing upwards into the taller well leaved trees one can often spot the bright yellow breasts of these birds. They roam about in pairs or in small parties. The call note is rather a curious one and once learned it may be realised that the bird is quite common.

Other habits:—Mr. Stuart Baker gives the following excellent account of the habits.

"It is a familiar little bird, haunting gardens, orchards and the outskirts of villages as well as the fringe of forests and scrub-jungle. In the breeding season it performs wonderful acrobatic feats, darting up into the air and then with all its feathers, especially those of the rump, puffed out, it comes spinning down in a spiral to the perch it has left. Arrived there it spreads and flirts its tail like a little peacock, drooping its wings and uttering all the time a protracted, sibilant whistle or chirrup. It has a great variety of notes, the most striking of which is a prolonged "we-e-e-e-tu" a long, drawn-out wail with the last note dropping suddenly. This seems never to be uttered except in the rains, and when constantly repeated to the accompaniment of the splash and the sough of the wind, is one of the saddest little bird-notes imaginable. It is generally found in pairs and is not gregarious, though, where it is common, three or four may be seen together on the same tree, hunting actively for the insects which form its food."

"This makes a most exquisite and very small, deep cup-like nest which is placed in the fork of, or actually on, the bough of a small tree."

THE MALAYAN FAIRY BLUE-BIRD

Irena puella cyanea (Begbie.)

Description:—There is a very striking difference between the sexes of this bird but neither male nor female can be confused with any other local bird.

The male has only two colours in its plumage, bright, pale, shiny blue and deep velvety black.

The blue extends to the top of the head, back, upper wing-coverts and under and upper-tail coverts.

Except the wing and tail-quills which are mostly dull brown, the female is almost entirely blue but this is a very different blue from that of the male being dull and without the gloss and furthermore quite different in tone—a brownish blue rather than the lively bright colour of the male.

The irides are red and the bill and feet black.

Length 9 or 10 inches; wing about 5 inches.

Distribution:—Fairy blue-birds are found in India, the Indo-Chinese countries, the Philippines and throughout Malaysia.

Status in Singapore:—Not a common garden bird but preferring the quieter and well-wooded parts of the island. It is numerous on Bukit Timah and at Changi and common on Pulau Ubin.

Field Notes:—The bright colours of male are not evident at a very short distance and as the species keeps very much to large trees it is usually noticed as a dark somewhat thick-set bird bulking considerably larger than the bulbuls. In Singapore it is usually seen in pairs.

[179]

It is often detected by its beautiful rich notes which can be heard on the path winding to the top of Bukit Timah. The other sweet and arresting notes heard there are uttered by the shama (see page 192) and the king-crow or drongo (see page 200).

Other habits : —This is a fruit-eating bird and inhabits the forests rather than more open country. The nest is said to be a shallow cup of moss or twigs placed in a small tree.

The eggs, usually two, are greenish white washed with brown.

Drawn by G. A. Levett-Yeats.

THE YELLOW-VENTED BULBUL.

Pycnonotus goiavier analis.

THE YELLOW-VENTED BULBUL

Pycnonotus goiavier analis (Horsf.)

Malay name: —Měrěbah.

Description: —The upper parts are brown darker on the head and the feathers, particularly of the wing, with slightly paler (or olive brown) edges. There is a conspicuous white stripe over the eye and the chin and throat are also white. The breast and abdomen are dirty white strongly washed with brown and faintly streaked with the same colour. Under-tail coverts yellow.

The iris is brown, the beak and feet black.

Length 8 inches, wing 3½ inches.

The sexes are alike in plumage but young birds are more dingy in colour.

Distribution: —*Pycnonotus goiavier* is found in the Philippine Islands but its Malayan representative, our own familiar yellow-vented bulbul, is found throughout the Malaysian islands and is a common bird in the Malay Peninsula and even further north in Tenasserim, etc.

Status in Singapore: —One of the commonest and most noticeable birds on the island and found almost everywhere except in places like Raffles Square or Battery Road but even there one has only to walk to the nearest green patch (the Cricket Club ground) to see it.

It nests freely in many parts of the island and particularly in the town gardens.

Field Notes: —In the field this very common bird, at the short distance at which it can usually be observed, appears to be pale brown in colour, rather darker on the back, with a white head and a pale yellow patch under the tail. When it nods its head a brown or blackish patch can be seen on the crown. It has no song worth mentioning but it is nevertheless rarely silent, its cheery chattering in the shrubs being continually in one's ears.

Other habits:—The cup-shaped nests which in Singapore are made, and in some years contain eggs, as early as the second half of February are easy enough to find and a good many bulbuls breed each year in the Botanic Gardens. The nests are usually placed in a bush (often an isolated one growing on a lawn) or in a hedge surrounding a tennis court. Two eggs are laid. They have the ground colour white, perhaps tinged with pink, and marked either with bold blotches or less well-defined splashes and speckled with some shade of brown. The eggs in fact are very variable in colour.

To a large extent the food consists of insects and berries and Ridley quite rightly remarks that: "it is an omnivorous bird, devouring small fruits of all kinds, especially those of the Waringin (*Ficus benjamina*) and the cinnamons, and is very troublesome when the fruit is wanted for any purpose, often clearing the whole tree and disseminating seeds in all kinds of places, where young trees come up in the most unexpected manner. It, however, atones for the trouble it gives to some extent by destroying a good many injurious insects such as grasshoppers and termites".

THE LARGE OLIVE BULBUL

Pycnonotus plumosus plumosus (Blyth)

Description:—This is a very soberly-clad bird with scarcely any distinguishing feature. It is about the size of the last-named and more familiar bird, *P. analis*. In the field it just appears to be of a darkish brown colour. In the hand it will be seen that the top of the head is brownish grey, the upper parts olive brown, the wings and tail strongly washed with dull green. The entire underparts are pale brown except the under-tail coverts which are yellowish brown.

The sexes are alike. The irides are reddish brown, the bill black and the feet brown.

Length nearly 8 inches; wing $3\frac{1}{4}$ or $3\frac{1}{2}$ inches.

Distribution:—This bird is found in the Malay Peninsula, where it is a common bird, and through the Malaysian Islands.

Status in Singapore:—This is a common bulbul and indeed in the mangrove areas and such spots as the Bukit Timah jungle it outnumbers the yellow-vented bulbul. It rarely comes into the town gardens but prefers the coast districts: we have seen it at odd times in the Botanic Gardens although even here it keeps to the shady wooded corners, not appearing in domestic fashion on the lawns and roads as does the ubiquitous *P. analis*.

It breeds on the island.

Habits:—The nest is placed in bushes only a few feet above the ground. Nests have been found in the Botanic Gardens, (Ridley mentions one close to the ground in some ferns) but this is perhaps rather unusual and the species is rather more a bird of the forests.

[183]

Allied species

Three other olive-brown bulbuls in size more or less the same as *P. plumosus* are not uncommon in Singapore but they are essentially country birds and do not normally approach the town.

They all differ from *P. plumosus* in lacking the green wash on the wings. These three species are Moore's olive bulbul (*Pycnonotus simplex*) with white irides, Blyth's olive bulbul (*P. brunneus*) with orange or reddish irides and a slightly smaller species with a smaller and blacker bill and also with red irides which may be known as the small olive bulbul (*P. erythropthalmos*).

We have obtained all these birds on Bukit Timah on the same day. *P. erythropthalmos* seems to be the least common of the three.

[184]

BABBLERS

Timaliidæ

GENERAL remarks about the birds of this family are rather difficult to make without resorting to a vagueness bordering on the dishonest. The guide to the bird galleries in the British Museum, which book we have found very useful in writing these introductory bits dealing with "orders" and "families", does not help us much at this point for it says that: "the characters and limits of this large Old World family, which includes a somewhat varied assemblage of species, are still imperfectly understood".

Be that as it may the babblers have certain points in common that bind them together. They differ from the bulbuls in that the legs are stronger and comparatively longer.

They are rarely truly arboreal in habit but in many cases are shy little birds, never flying further than possible and preferring to slip about through the undergrowth near the ground. The wings are usually small and somewhat concave: none of the approximately sixty Malayan species are migratory and the great majority are shy jungle birds. A few species are met with in country gardens; they are always scarce on small islands and in spite of the many kinds found in Malaya only two, and these are both mentioned below, can be considered as anything like familiar birds in Singapore.

THE BROWN-BACKED TIT-BABBLER

Malacocincla abbotti (Blyth)

Description:—This babbler which, in Singapore at least, is known far better by its note than by its appearance is a squat, short-necked little bird, with a very short tail and longish legs. In size it is rather larger than a sparrow.

There are few distinctive features about its plumage. The upper parts are entirely brown, and the lower parts whitish well-washed with rufous on the flanks and with the under tail coverts quite rich rufous.

The iris is reddish brown, the beak brown and grey and the legs fleshy in colour.

Length 6½ inches; wing 3 inches.

The sexes are alike.

Distribution:—This bird is found in parts of India, in Burma, Siam, etc. and through the Malay Peninsula to Sumatra and Borneo, although the birds from the latter locality are sufficiently distinct to merit recognition as a sub-species.

Status in Singapore:—A common bird breeding in the jungle at the Botanic Gardens but on account of its very skulking habits not often seen although its very distinctive call-note must be familiar to many.

Field Notes:—This babbler has a characteristic call note which can be most aptly written "What-you-doing". The words always seem to us as remarkably distinct. Although the bird is found during the day in thick cover, and always either alone or with its mate and young family, it seems to have a habit of getting up very early and making tours in somewhat unexpected districts.

[186]

Thus from the verandah of a house in Fort Canning Road we used often, in the early morning, to hear the quite unmistakable note of this species as one solitary bird worked its way from garden to garden down the road, no doubt to retire to a less populous area before the sun was very high. Likewise a friend of ours has noticed that in the early morning one or two of these birds will pass the Labrador Villa—calling to each other as they worked through the bushes and undergrowth fringing the coast. When once the bird is located it often allows a close approach and then the feature that one can readily pick out of an otherwise dull picture is the somewhat rufous wash on the flanks which seems even more pronounced in a living bird than in a museum skin.

Other habits:—Although we have seen young birds being fed by their parents in the patch of jungle at the Botanic Gardens we have never found a nest. Mr. Stuart Baker writing of the bird's habits in India and Burma says: "It breeds only in deep, wet tree-forest with ample undergrowth and preferably near some stream, making a massive nest of dead leaves, weeds and grass with an inner cup of leaves, roots and weeds compactly bound together and lined with some fern-palm, near the ground. The eggs number three to five and are very beautiful, the ground-colour varies from a very pale to a rich pale salmon pink, whilst the markings consists of spots, blotches and lines of deep red-brown with paler spots of light red and neutral tint".

Of about the same size as *T. abbotti* is *Anuropsis malaccensis*. This babbler is furthermore very similar in plumage to *abbotti* but it may be distinguished by its even yet longer legs, the much whiter throat and the grey face. It is not uncommonly met with in those parts of the Botanic Gardens in which the vegetation is wild and thick and like *abbotti* it slips about the undergrowth and is of skulking habits. The voice is very characteristic and consists of a run of clear distinct whistles.

[187]

A third species of a like size and again very similar in plumage and habits to these two is *Aethostoma rostratum*. It is, however, a darker brown on the back and almost pure white below. It appears to be not uncommon on Pulau Ubin and we have seen it in the mangrove in Singapore.

Other Babblers

Only two other babblers deserves mention here. The yellow-breasted babbler, *Mixornis rubricapilla pileata* has the crown and the whole of the upper parts including the wings and tail brown tinged with rufous. The underparts are yellow, washed with dull green on the flanks and with the throat and breast streaked with thin, short, black marks. The length is just over 5 inches and the bird is thus "sparrow-size" or rather smaller. We have never seen it in the gardens or very near the town but in the country districts it is far from uncommon. It prefers the rough country, tall, tangled undergrowth and the jungle rather than the more open planted up areas. *Cyanoderma crythropterum* is a small brown bird with slaty-blue throat and breast and can be recognised by the bare areas of blue skin about the eyes. It is a forest dweller.

THRUSHES

Turdidæ

THIS family includes the familiar song-thrush or "mavis" and the blackbird of Europe as well as the smaller and equally well-known redstarts, stonechats and wheatears, etc.

All thrushes, whatever their adult plumage, are spotted when young and they furthermore differ from their nearest allies, the warblers, in that they have no spring moult.

Many of the species are beautiful songsters. Roughly thirty kinds have been recorded from the Malay Peninsula but a large percentage of these are not familiar birds and are not likely to be met with by the amateur.

The water-loving forktails (*Henicurinæ*) and the whistling thrushes (*Myiophoneus*) are not met with in Singapore where the magpie robin and the shama, both mentioned in greater detail below, are the only members of the family likely to be observed.

THE MAGPIE-ROBIN

Copsychus saularis musicus (Raffles)

Malay name : —Murai.

Description : —This is the sprightly black and white thrush-like bird so common in Singapore gardens.

The male has the upper parts together with the chin, throat and breast glossy black. The remainder of the under-parts are white. The wings have a broad white bar and the outer tail feathers are also white.

The female is scarcely so deep a black on the upper parts and the chin, throat and breast are grey instead of black.

Young birds are blackish-grey above and have the white bar on the wings and the grey breast mottled with yellowish-brown.

Irides brown, bill black, legs dark grey.

The bird runs to 9 inches in length with a wing of about 4 inches.

Distribution : —Forms of *Copsychus saularis* are found from Ceylon where, at Colombo, Straits residents going ashore from their boat can meet with this familiar bird, throughout India and thence up to China and down south through the Malay Peninsula and Malaysian Islands.

Status in Singapore : —The magpie-robin is so common in Singapore that it needs little mention under this heading. In the gardens it is one of the most familiar of birds and although it does not actually enter the busy parts of the town like the tree-sparrow and the yellow-vented bulbul, it is common enough on the outskirts and in most other places to attract notice.

It breeds freely on the island.

[190]

THE MAGPIE ROBIN.
Copsycus saularis musicus.

Drawn by G. A. Levett-Yeats.

Field Notes:—This bird is not only of thrush size but also very thrush-like in its actions. It hops about the lawns and tennis courts in a bold and confident manner, regales us with wonderful music when the spirit moves it and provides ample amusement when the males are assiduously courting the hens and singing one against the other with such goodwill that we often pause to wonder that they find it worth while!

Other habits:—The murai makes a large cup-like nest of grass which is placed in the fork of a smallish tree, or in the Botanic Gardens very frequently in a palm in which case the nest is wedged in between the stalk-leaf and the stem of the palm. According to Ridley nests are sometimes placed on a beam beneath the verandah of a house.

[With the black and white plumage of a magpie and the confiding habits and jerky movements of a robin this engaging bird is probably the best known in the Island. It may be seen in most gardens, either on the lawn or perched on a branch or on the verandah rail uttering its very melodious and charming though short song. It also frequents the less dense jungle in rural districts but has no fear of man and is a favourite and tame cage bird. It is very pugnacious and bold and has royal battles with its brothers.

It has a curious habit of sharply raising and lowering its tail just as does a robin or English hedge-sparrow. It feeds on worms and insects: it properly nests in thick shrubs but often builds almost anywhere; in a hollow stump used for training orchids, in an old tin, in a hole in a wall, under the eaves of a house and even in a constantly used stable; about four eggs are as a rule laid of a pale-blue ground colour blotched and spotted with brown.—J. A. S. B.].

THE SHAMA

Kittacincla malabarica tricolor (Vieill.)

Malay name : —Murai batu.

Description : —The shama is a striking and handsome bird, very like the magpie-robin in shape but with a much longer tail.

The male has the head, neck, back and wings shining black, the rump pure white and the breast and abdomen deep chestnut. The tail is black and white. The colours do not merge into each other but join in sharply defined lines. A straight line across the lower throat marks the black and chestnut zones and another line on the lower back separates the white rump from the black back.

Females are not so bright as the males; the chestnut of the underparts being replaced by rich yellowish-brown. The tail is also shorter.

The iris is brown, the bill black and the feet pale fleshy colour.

In the male, the total length is about 11 inches and the wing $3\frac{3}{4}$ inches.

Distribution : —The shama is found in India, the Indo-Chinese countries, the Malay Peninsula and thence throughout the islands of Borneo, Sumatra, Java, etc. Other members of the genus occur in the Philippines.

Status in Singapore : —The shama is not uncommon in Singapore, but it is much more retiring in its habits than the magpie-robin, being found in the thick woods rather than the open country. Birds may often be seen in the Botanic Gardens but even in this limited environment they display their natural preference for seclusion, sulking among the undergrowth or in the jungle rather than appearing on the paths and lawns. Their presence is usually betrayed by their most beautiful voice.

[192]

Ridley, drawing his conclusions from the somewhat uncertain appearance of the species in the gardens, thought that it was migratory and indeed it does appear, like many other local species, to be subject to movements of a kind; but a certain number of shamas are certainly resident on the island and some breed on Bukit Timah.

Field Notes:—This bird is one of the most beautiful of our local songsters. Its voice resembles in a very large degree that of the magpie-robin but is even more varied, richer and louder. Seen at a distance it rather resembles its commoner relative, but at close quarters the chestnut underparts and longer tail are distinctive.

Other habits:—Mr. Stuart Baker writes: "The Malayan Shama breeds in March, April and May, placing its nest in holes in trees or in bamboo clumps. It is always very roughly built of twigs, leaves and grass, lined with grass and fits into the hollow in which it is built. The eggs number three or four, and are very like those of the Dayal [*i.e.* the magpie-robin] but usually much more densely spotted and therefore more brown in general tint".

The shama is an insectivorous bird. Ridley states that if one whistles the first few bars of its song, the bird may be drawn to the edge of the wood, coming quite close to the observer and pouring forth its melodious song.

WARBLERS

Sylviidæ

THE warblers are small birds usually of plainly coloured plumage. They are frequently very fine singers and it may be noted that that expert performer the blackcap is a warbler. Other well-known European members of the family are the white-throats and the reed and sedge warblers. In Malaya the most noticeable warblers are the tiny tailor-birds so very remarkable by reason of their wonderful nests which are literally sewn together, and for their calls, of a loudness out of all proportion to the size of these birds.

Drawn by G. A. Levett-Yeats.

THE BLACK-NECKED TAILOR-BIRD.
Orthotomus atrigularis.

THE BLACK-NECKED TAILOR-BIRD

Orthotomus atrogularis (Temm.)

Description:—The top of the head chestnut, the upper parts green, lower parts white with the throat and fore-neck black.

The female has no black on the throat, etc. and young males often have these parts not wholly black but streaked with white.

The irides are yellowish-brown and the bill and feet brown.

This small species is usually about $4\frac{1}{2}$ to 5 inches in length and has a wing of approximately $1\frac{3}{4}$ inches.

Distribution:—The black-necked tailor-bird is found from Northern India to Annam and t' ence southward to Sumatra and Borneo.

Status in Singapore:—One of the common garden birds of the island and a cheery little fellow usually seen flitting about the bushes in a confiding manner in well-populated places.

Other habits:—The tailor-birds of course owe their trivial name to the skill with which they construct their nests. A large leaf is curled round and the edges drawn together by means of regular stitches of fibre, or any convenient sewing material that happens to be handy when nest building is in process.

Within the neat receptable thus formed the actual nest is placed. In some nests in the Raffles Museum (although we are by no means sure that they belong to *O. atrogularis*) the receptable is formed not of one large curled leaf, but of two leaves stitched together at the edges. One has to examine a tailor-birds nest to appreciate the ingenuity shown in its construction. In some examples the tailoring is better than in others, but all show the holes made along the edges of the leaf through which is threaded the substitute for the tailor's thread.

[195]

Other Tailor-birds

Another species of tailor-bird is found commonly in the country districts of Singapore, but it is scarcely as numerous as the last species and unlike that bird it rarely appears in the town gardens. This second kind may be known as the ashy tailor-bird (*O. sepium cineraceus*). In general appearance it is ashy-grey, rather more brownish on the wings and tail and the feathers of the latter having small black and white tips. The abdomen is whitish and the thighs are chestnut. The characteristic feature of the plumage is that the chin as well as the top and sides of the head is also chestnut. The female has the rufous on the head less pronounced.

Yet a third species of *Orthotomus*, the red-headed tailor-bird (*O. ruficeps*) is not rare in the country districts of Singapore, and indeed common on the outlying islands. This is rather larger than the two already described. It has the top of the head chestnut, the entire underparts white, the back and wings grey and the tail reddish-brown.

The tailor-birds are all very similar in habits.

SHRIKES

Laniidæ

THE true shrikes, or butcher-birds, are found in most parts of the world but not in South America. They are mostly small birds in which the young differ in plumage from the adults, the immature plumage being barred.

They are carnivorous in diet but whereas the smaller species, as might be expected, feed mainly on insects, the larger kinds vary their diet with mice, birds, lizards, etc. In plumage the shrikes exhibit a considerable range of colouring: some species are arrayed in vivid colours while others are characterised by their sombre dress.

The beak is hooked somewhat in the manner of a falcon. Most country people are familiar with the curious habits of the red-backed shrike which impales its prey on thorns, the accumulated food eventually forming a regular larder. Five members of the genus *Lanius* are recorded from the Malay Peninsula.

THE THICK-BILLED SHRIKE

Lanius tigrinus (*Drap.*)

Description:—Although we describe the adult plumage of this bird by far the large majority of the individuals of this species seen in Singapore are in immature plumage and this differs rather considerably from that of the adult.

The old bird has the top of the head and a portion of the back grey, the rest of the upper parts very rich brown, almost chestnut, barred with black and the underparts white. The space between the eye and the bill together with a large patch behind the eye is black.

The young bird has all the upper parts rich brown barred with black and the underparts white, likewise irregularly barred with blackish. This is the plumage in which the species is usually met with in Singapore although a fair number of the birds seen indicate the approach of the mature plumage in that they have lost the barring on the head.

The irides are brown, the beak and feet slaty.

Length about 6½ inches, wing just over 3 inches.

Habits:—The thick-billed shrike breeds in Northern China and Japan wintering in South China, the Malay Peninsula, etc. In Singapore it is usually seen in the autumn and winter months and a favourite perch is one of the posts supporting the netting round a tennis court.

In addition to the thick-billed shrike, other closely allied shrikes appear occasionally as migrants in Singapore: these include the Philippine shrike (*Lanius cristatus luconiensis*), the brown shrike (*L. c. cristatus*) and the chestnut-crowned shrike (*L. c. superciliosus*) all of which are sub-species of the same bird, breeding in different areas to the north of Singapore but mixing together when they reach their winter quarters.

They are all about the same in size and very similar in appearance.

DRONGOS

Dicruridæ

THE drongos or king-crows are found in Africa and also in India and thence east throughout the Malaysian area to Australia. They are usually of glossy black plumage and the tail is frequently forked. Their method of catching their insect food is very much like that of the flycatchers, the birds waiting on some convenient perch and then darting forth into the air and returning to the same perch when the prey is captured. In addition to the more typical black drongos several grey birds are known from Malaysia but none of these occur in Singapore whence, in addition to that dealt with below only two other species have been recorded. These are the crow-billed drongo (*Dicrurus annectens*) which is a winter-visitor to Malaysia and the Malayan bronzed drongo (*Chaptia ænea malayensis*) but both of these must be rare and they have not been met with in recent years.

THE LARGER RACQUET-TAILED DRONGO

Dissemurus paradiseus platurus (Vieill.)

Malay name :—Chĕchawi; Hamba kĕra.

Description :—The most characteristic feature of this small crow-like bird is the enormous lengthening of the two outer tail quills. These are continued beyond the ends of the other tail feathers as long thin shafts, at the extremities of which is a large curled "blob" of feather vane—a feature well represented in our plate. The entire plumage is glossy black but if the bird is held in the hand bluish reflections can be seen.

The bill and feet are black; the iris is dark red.

Total length to the end of the normal tail feathers 12 inches, including the tail "wires" 23 inches : wing 6½ inches.

Distribution :—The racquet-tailed drongo is found in Ceylon, India, Burma, Hainan and thence south to the Malay Peninsula and the Malaysian Islands; but within this area it is easy to recognise several races or sub-species, the birds from different countries showing considerable variation in size and also in the character of the crest and tail. The actual race (*platurus*) found in Singapore occurs only in the southern part of the Malay Peninsula and Sumatra.

[*Status in Singapore :*—This black bird with its immensely long tail is common enough in the wooded parts of Singapore Island, such as near Changi or in the Jurong area.

Field Notes and Habits :—This bird is usually seen alone or in pairs flying from tree to tree. When flying it really looks as if the bird was trailing behind it a long piece of thin black ribbon with a widened tip : once seen it can never be forgotten. Its usual note is a loud, shrill series of high calls but it is said to imitate in a wild state many other birds' notes in great variety. It feeds on insects which it captures as a rule on

Drawn by G. A. Levett Yeats.

THE LARGER RACQUET-TAILED DRONGO.
Dissemurus paradisus platurus.

THE LARGER RACQUET-TAILED DRONGO

the wing: it is stated to be hardy, tame and an excellent mimic in captivity producing all sorts of noises such as barking, mewing, crowing and so forth as well as singing beautifully. It makes a clumsy nest in, as a rule, the branches of a tree and lays about three, usually, pinkish-white eggs spotted with reddish purple.—J. A. S. B.].

STARLINGS

Sturnidæ

THE starlings, which for the sake of simplicity are here treated as one group, are sometimes divided into two families the first of which, the tree-starlings, are arboreal in habits and characterised by laying spotted eggs. The tree-starlings include the mynas or grackles which are well-known as cage-birds and on account of the parrot-like ability of certain individuals to imitate the human voice.

The true starlings which form the second family are more terrestrial in habits and the eggs are unspotted: only three species are found in the southern part of the Malay Peninsula and are by no means familiar birds.

Drawn by G. A. Levett-Yeats.

THE JAVAN HILL-MYNAH.
Gracula javana.

THE MALAYAN GRACKLE

Gracula javana javana (Osbeck)

Malay name:—Tiong.

Description:—The grackle, the shape of which can be seen by reference to our plate is entirely glossy bluish-black in plumage except for a small white patch on the wing quills.

Touches of colour are provided by the soft parts in that the bill is orange with a yellow tip, and the feet are bright yellow as are also the fleshy lappets that adorn the nape. The iris is brown.

Length about 12 inches, wing between 6½ to 7 inches.

The metallic reflections of the plumage are only seen when the bird is closely examined. Even in the hand the plumage appears entirely black when held at arms length.

In the plate the reflections are rather too pronounced.

Distribution:—The tiong is found in the Malay Peninsula, Borneo, Sumatra and Java. The birds found in India, China, the Philippines and even as far east as the islands of Flores and Sumbawa are very closely allied and probably no more than local races of the one species.

Status in Singapore:—A common bird but not a frequenter of the town. In the country districts and even in the Botanic Gardens it may be seen.

Field Notes:—The tiong is perhaps best known as he sits high up, on a tall tree, more often than not on the topmost branch and sends forth, especially in the early morning, the far reaching *"ti-ong"* in the form of clear notes. In the evening small flocks may be noticed as the birds fly to roost and at a distance the compact little bands may be mistaken for green pigeon. In flight the birds appear quite black except for a conspicuous white patch in each wing.

Other habits:—This is a favourite cage-bird with the natives and some examples are quite good talkers and can also learn to imitate other sounds such as the human cough.

A hole in a dead tree, very often high up, seems to be the favourite nesting site.

Drawn by G. A. Levett-Yeats.

THE MALAYAN GLOSSY TREE-STARLING.

Lamprocorax panayensis strigata.

THE GLOSSY TREE-STARLING

Aplonis panayensis strigatus (Horsf.)

Description:—Few of our local birds exhibit such an enormous difference in plumage dependent on age than does this tree-starling. Adults of both sexes have the entire plumage an extremely dark glossy green.

Bill and feet partake of the general dark tone in that they are black but the eye is crimson.

In young birds the underparts are creamy white with bold greenish-black streaks and the iris is yellowish-white.

The total length is about 8½ inches and the wing measures just over 4 inches.

Distribution:—This species in various forms, is found throughout Malaysia and also in India. A critical examination of all the known members of the genus would no doubt greatly extend this range as birds from countries much further east seem to be but local representatives of *A. panayensis*.

Status in Singapore:—A certain number of these tree-starlings are undoubtedly resident in the district but the huge numbers that appear when certain trees are fruiting are not always with us. Large flocks are common in the autumn and winter.

Field Notes:—The very noisy flocks of birds that congregate on house-tops and in trees actually within the city of Singapore are usually of this species. At a distance of a few yards the old birds appear to be quite black with conspicuous *red* eyes and the young birds streaked.

[205]

[*Other habits*:—In Singapore numerically much stronger than the mynah or grackle. It is found in considerable flocks even in the city where dozens may often be seen perched on such eminences as the spire of the old Armenian Church or the trees near the Chinese Protectorate. In gardens it descends like the locust on fruit trees such as the Jambu and commits great havoc, but it also eats insects.—J. A. S. B.].

WEAVER-FINCHES

Ploceidæ

THIS is a large family of small birds, superficially very like the finches and buntings but distinguished by certain structural differences. Several members of the genus *Munia* are very common in Singapore but these do not display the same skill in the construction of their nests as does the common weaver-bird (*Ploceus passerinus infortunatus*) which is, however, not at all common in Singapore and can only be accorded passing notice. For the greater part of the year both sexes are dull insignificant-looking birds, in size and general appearance not unlike the hen sparrow of English towns. The upper parts are brown with copious dark streaks and the underparts very pale uniform brown or buff. The male, however, has a more resplendent dress which he wears in the summer, but loses again at the autumn moult. In this plumage the top of the head is bright yellow and the chin and throat are very dark brown.

The bottle-shaped nest composed of very closely woven-grass is suspended (by the "neck") from a twig and although apparently insecure, swaying in the breeze, it is almost impossible to detach the nest from its supports without tearing it to pieces.

THE JAVA SPARROW

Munia orizivora (Linn.)

Malay name : —Jĕlatek.

Description : —At a distance of a few yards this appears to be a small bird of about sparrow size and almost entirely pale, delicate grey in colour but with a black and white head.

The upper parts of the head, the chin and the tail are black; the sides of the head white. All the rest of the plumage is pale grey except the abdomen which is dull pink becoming whitish in the centre.

The sexes are similar in plumage and run to about $5\frac{1}{2}$ inches in length with a wing of about $2\frac{3}{4}$ inches.

The iris is red and the feet and bill pink.

Distribution : —Owing to the fact that this is a very common cage-bird being kept not only by natives in the east but also commonly imported into other parts of the world it is rather difficult to decide as to the natural range of the species. It is common in Java, Sumatra and the Malay Peninsula.

[The Java sparrow is very common in the neighbourhood of Singapore and with its bright red beak, dove grey plumage and white cheeks is no doubt familiar to everyone. It is known also as the rice-bird and sometimes as the paddy-bird.

Very noisy and pugnacious it behaves much like the ordinary sparrow squatting and chattering round the eaves and roofs of houses which it fancies and unlike most weavers not suspending its nest from a branch, but building a round structure in a tree or even in a recess in the ornamental masonry of a private dwelling : it lays white eggs. It is caught and exposed for sale in hundreds in the bird-shops where it can be bought for a few cents. Though often kept it is rather a nuisance in an aviary as it worries other birds and tears up their attempts

Drawn by G. A. Levett-Yeats.

THE JAVA SPARROW.
Munia oryzivora.

at nest making. It is primarily a grain feeder but will eat almost anything. It is a very vigorous personality and is extending its range having in comparatively recent years established itself—possibly originally as an escape—in parts of Southern India.—J. A. S. B.].

THE WHITE-HEADED MUNIA

Munia maja (Linn.)

Malay name:—Pipit uban.

Description:—This bird is known to Europeans in Singapore as the "Cigar-bird" and indeed this is an excellent name, for the little brown bird with its white head and neck is strangely reminiscent of a partly smoked cigar.

The sexes are alike: both have the head and neck and throat white, the upper parts chestnut, much brighter on the rump and tail. The underparts are also dull brownish chestnut but with black on the centre of the breast and abdomen: the under tail-coverts black.

The irides are brown; the bill and feet bright slate colour.

Total length is from 4 to 4½ inches; wing about 2¼ inches.

Distribution:—This bird is found only in the Malay Peninsula, Sumatra and Java.

[It goes about in flocks and is perhaps most often noticed hopping about on the grass of lawns not too closely cut and makes rather a comical figure: the little parties jump up when disturbed and go off like a lot of big bees or tiny quail with straight flight and feeble squeaks. It is caught in great numbers and is a common cage-bird. It feeds on rice and seeds and makes its nest in reeds or high grasses laying several white eggs.—J. A. S. B.].

Several other species of *Munia* are common in Singapore and indeed some of them are quite as often seen as *M. maja* and only consideration of space has induced us to select one species, almost at random, to figure and describe.

If the white head and neck of the birds in our plate could be changed to black the figures would do equally well for the chestnut-bellied munia (*M. atricapilla*) which is common in Singapore frequenting the same kind of ground and displaying

Drawn by G. A. Levett-Yeats.

THE WHITE-HEADED MUNIA.
Munia maja.

almost the same habits as *M. maja* except for the fact that it does not seem to congregate into such huge flocks and that it is furthermore rather partial to the outlying islands.

The young of both species are very much alike and could not be identified in the field. Both are brown above and pale brown below: they also lack the characteristic white or black head.

Two other species somewhat alike in plumage are quite numerous locally and are to be seen on the lawns of the Botanic Gardens. These are even rather smaller than the two munias mentioned above. The upper parts are quite dark brown and indeed black on the tail, the throat and breast are dark brown or black and the abdomen white or pale grey. Of these two birds, the Javan white-breasted munia (*M. leucogaster*) has the upper parts more or even uniform, the breast quite black and the abdomen really white: Hodgson's munia (*M. acuticauda*) has a whitish rump, conspicuous when the bird flits a few paces and the breast "scale-like", an effect produced by the pale edges of the dark feathers: the abdomen is greyish.

Yet one more species deserves mention on account of its abundance on the island. Broadly speaking the spotted munia (*M. punctulata*) is entirely pale chestnut except on the breast and abdomen where this species differs from all the other local members of the genus in having these parts white with all the feathers broadly edged with chestnut. At a distance of a few yards the underparts appear boldly spotted (or irregularly barred) brown and white.

FINCHES AND BUNTINGS

Fringillidæ

ONLY three of the very large number of species (about six hundred) included in this family are found in the Malay Peninsula and of these one is confined to the high mountains and another is only met with in the north of the Peninsula and then only in the winter.

The finches and buntings are typically small seed-eating birds with a short strong bill.

Drawn by G. A. Levett-Yeats.

THE ORIENTAL TREE-SPARROW.

Passer montanus malaccensis,

THE MALAYAN TREE SPARROW

Passer montanus malaccensis (Dubois)

Malay name :—Pipit.

Description :—The plumage of the local tree sparrow is to all intents and purposes the same as that of the familiar tree-sparrow of the English lanes.

The top of the head is chestnut, the upper parts pale brown streaked with dark brown and black. The chin and throat are black forming a "bib" : the lower parts are greyish tinged here and there with pale brown.

The female is like the male.

The irides are brown, the bill black and the feet pale brown.

Length between 5½ and 6 inches; wing 2½ inches.

Distribution :—The Malayan tree-sparrow is found only in Malaysia but the sparrows of China, Siberia and Japan are very closely allied indeed and both these forms are yet again very little different from the tree-sparrow of Europe of which latter species they are but certainly only local races.

[The house sparrow of Europe is in most far Eastern countries replaced by some kind of so-called tree-sparrow which though it seems to hold the field where it occurs is not so pugnacious or noisy as the "feathered rat" of England. Owing to slight variations in plumage due no doubt to geographical separation experts recognise several sub-species, of which the Malayan bird is one. In England where it is pretty common it nests in trees and does not frequent houses in the same way as does its there more abundant cousin : and hence no doubt its name : but in Singapore it has all the habits of its ally and may be seen and heard everywhere—on house-tops, on the road, in farm yards and so forth—and is rather a nuisance : it will also nest almost anywhere and eat almost anything. The nest is the usual clumsy untidy mass of straw and feathers, paper and string and it lays usually five or six white eggs speckled or splashed in a much varying degree with dark spots and marks. Sometimes it will live at some houses quite amicably with the Java sparrow but if there are, as often is the case, disputes the latter is master.—J. A. S. B.].

SUNBIRDS

Nectariniidæ

In their general appearance the sunbirds bear a strong resemblance to the humming-birds and it is not unusual to find that the two families are frequently confused by laymen.

The humming-birds however are not even "perching-birds" (*Passeriformes*) and are therefore quite unrelated to the sunbirds. They are placed by systematists in that miscellaneous Order the Coraciiformes. Humming-birds are only found in the New World and sunbirds only in the Old World.

In the sunbirds the plumage is frequently very beautiful and metallic in character; but the sexes are usually quite distinct, only the males being brilliantly clad the females more often than not being arrayed in sober greens, greys and yellows.

By means of the tongue which is very long and tubular, the birds as they flit from bush to bush like honey bees, extract nectar from the flowers. It is frequently asserted that the sunbirds cannot hover or remain poised over a flower as can the humming-birds but this is not strictly true for occasionally we have seen them hovering like a hawk-moth over a bloom: normally they cling to the stem of the flower they feed from, or to some other handy support.

In their nesting habits they display features of very great interest some of which are noticed under the specific headings.

The sunbirds are all of small size: the family is divided into two sub-families, the one including the true or typical sunbirds and the other the spider-hunters in which the plumage is duller, like that of the female sunbirds. Both sub-families are extremely well represented in the Malay Peninsula, the sunbirds by thirteen and the spider-hunters by seven species. A fair number of these, all mentioned below, occur in Singapore but some are not common.

In one respect the typical sunbirds are the easiest group with which we have to deal but in other respects they are far the most difficult. The males of all the species are quite unmistakable and a very brief description should enable the reader to recognise them in the field. The females on the other hand are as difficult to recognise as the males are easy and at a short distance they all look very much alike. So convinced are we of the futility of attempting to give hints for their recognition in the field that we have paid scant attention to the matter. In their general appearance sunbirds are rather characteristic and reference to our plate of one of the common species will be of more help to the reader than many written words. Note the small size and the sickle shaped bill: the birds on the plate are drawn about rather more than two-thirds of the natural size and represent the largest of the local common species.

Three species are very common in Singapore, two others are less common but by no means rare.

The field points of the males are: —

Chalcostetha calcostetha.—Appears all black at the distance of a few yards except for two bright yellow tufts on the sides best seen when the wings are open. Usually seen in mangrove.

Anthreptes malaccensis.—Metallic purple and green above but dark at a short distance. Throat brown, remainder of underparts yellow. Uusually seen in coconut land but also in gardens and woodlands.

Leptocoma ornata.—Upper parts greenish, lower parts bright yellow. Throat very dark metallic blue (black at a few yards). The common sunbird of Singapore gardens.

[216]

Leptocoma brasiliana.—Top of the head green, throat magenta. Upper parts black, lower parts *very* dark red. Found in the mangrove and countryside but not in the town gardens and not very common.

Aethopyga siparaja.—A bright red jewel-like bird; red above and below except on the abdomen where it is smoky black. Like the petals of a hibiscus: yellow rump and dark blue tail. Common in gardens.

The females of all these species are very much alike. All are yellowish or yellowish-green below and greenish above *L. ornata* is the most distinctive of the lot in that the underparts are bright pure yellow. The female *C. calcostetha* has the throat whitish.

MAKLOT'S SUNBIRD

Chalcostetha calcostetha calcostetha (Jard.)

Description:—The male has the top of the head metallic green, sides of the head and the back black; the wing-coverts, lower back, rump and tail metallic violet or green and the wing-quills brownish black. On the underparts the chin and throat are metallic brownish-red or perhaps "copper-colour" is a better term to use here, the breast metallic blue, abdomen black and a conspicuous tuft of bright yellow feathers on each side of the body.

In the female the top of the head is grey, the back and wings dull green: the tail all black but some of the feathers are tipped with white. The chin and throat dirty white; breast and abdomen yellow but not very bright.

The iris is brown and the bill and feet black.

Length about 5½ inches; wing just less than 2½ inches.

Distribution:—From the south of Tenasserin and Siam down the Malay Peninsula to Borneo, Sumatra and other Malaysian islands.

Status in Singapore:—Although not met with in the gardens and in such localities as Bukit Timah and also generally speaking not in the woodlands, this is a common species in the mangrove and at various points along the coast. It is particularly numerous on the small islands lying just off the coast of Singapore but not only is this species local in its distribution but it is undoubtedly subject to a certain amount of local shifting for sometimes it will be very common in selected places and will then in a few weeks disappear.

Kelham wrote, "Swarms wherever there are coconut plantations, particularly if they be on the sea-shore. During September 1879, I saw literally hundreds of these Honeysuckers among the coconut trees at Tanjong Katong, Singapore."

One August we found this species extremely numerous on Pulau Merambong, the males predominating. The birds were evidently attracted to this tiny island by the flowering of the mangrove, the whole of the sea-shore being lined with the bright red blossoms.

Along the banks of creeks in Singapore it is also common.

Field Notes:—The best way to see the species is to visit Pulau Ubin and work round the shore for it is very common there. The male looks quite black at a distance of a few yards and cannot be mistaken.

Other habits:—Very little seems to have been published concerning the habits of this sunbird, a circumstance no doubt due to the fact that it is not found in India, and has therefore escaped the attention of the numerous good field naturalists who have written of so many birds common to India and Malaya.

THE PURPLE-HEADED SUNBIRD

Aethopygia siparaja siparaja (Horsf.)

Description:—The male of this most wonderful little bird cannot be confused with any other local species.

The head, neck, back, upper-wing coverts, chin, throat and breast are crimson. The throat and breast are rather brighter than the upper parts and could almost be called vermillion. The rump provides a dazzling contrast to the red colour in that it is yellow and this again gives way to dark metallic blue on the upper tail coverts and tail. The wings are dark brown and the abdomen slaty black.

The female is mostly dull green, slightly more yellowish on the underparts and in her dowdy dress forms a striking contrast to her gorgeous mate.

The young males are at first very like the females in general appearance and present a curious appearance when assuming the adult plumage as the red feathers appear here and there among the green ones.

The male measures about $4\frac{1}{4}$ to $4\frac{1}{2}$ inches in length and has a wing of just over 2 inches.

The irides, feet and beak are dark brown.

Distribution:—This sunbird reaches its northern limit at about the latitude of Penang, but it is common throughout the Malay Peninsula: found also in Borneo, Sumatra and Java: allied sub-species are found to the northwards from China to India.

Status in Singapore:—A common bird in most parts of the island, especially numerous in the woodlands at such places as Bukit Timah, the Changi jungle and also near Chinese market gardens. Very numerous on the outlying islands. It is also found in Singapore gardens, but never so numerously as the small yellow-breasted species next to be described.

Field Notes:—This is a confiding little bird usually allowing a close approach on the part of the observer. The red colour immediately distinguishes the male but it would be very difficult, if not impossible, to distinguish between the females of *A. siparaja* and *Leptocoma brasiliana* in the field.

Other habits:—This bird feeds on the nectar of *Canna* flowers and like other sunbirds will puncture the flower at the base in order to get at the sweet food. It also eats insects and is fond of spiders. Mr. Jacobson of Sumatra notes that the species is to be found wherever *Eugenia malaccensis* is flowering.

We have seen nestlings of this species taken in Singapore but have never found a nest.

It is interesting to note that this bird is characteristic of the lowlands wherever it is found and that in the mountains, roughly speaking above 3,000 feet, its place is taken by an allied species *A. temmincki*.

This is very much like *siparaja* in general appearance but perhaps on account of its much paler underparts it is even more beautiful. *A. temmincki* is common near the Gunong Angsi bungalow in Negri Sembilan.

THE MALAYAN YELLOW-BREASTED SUNBIRD

Leptocoma jugularis ornata (Less.)

Description:—The male has the forehead, throat and breast dark metallic blue, the upper parts and wings greenish (olive) and the abdomen bright yellow. The tail is almost black with the outer tail feathers partly white.

The female lacks the metallic blue parts of the male and is entirely greenish above and yellow below.

The soft parts display no conspicuous colours, the irides being dark brown and the beak and feet dark brown or black.

This is a tiny bird with a total length of about 4 inches or a little more and the wing usually just over 2 inches.

Distribution:—A common bird in the Malay Peninsula but replaced in the northern parts by a slightly altered sub-species.

It is also found in the Philippines, Borneo, Sumatra and Java and further afield the birds of Celebes and yet more to the east could perhaps be linked up as forms of this species.

Status in Singapore:—This is the common sunbird of the town gardens: it breeds freely even within the environs of the busy city and is found all over the island.

Field Notes:—In the Botanic Gardens the brilliant little male of this species should soon be found and recognised on account of his bright yellow underparts with neatly divided gorget of shining black. He may be looked for among the cannas, but most residents already know this bird by sight on account of its boldness in flying on to the verandahs of our houses, where it hangs to the chick cords (sometimes upside down!) and gazes around perhaps making a very thorough inspection of the ceiling and being rewarded with sundry unsuspecting spiders.

Other habits :—The nest is like an elongated pear in shape and is suspended by its thin end to the end of a bough sometimes many feet from the ground or on the other hand perhaps placed in a low bush where its conspicuous size and shape are at once responsible for its destruction. Nests are also commonly attached to convenient spots on the outside of occupied bungalows.

THE BROWN-THROATED SUNBIRD

Anthreptes malaccensis malaccensis (Scop.)

Description:—Here again we have a case in which the sexes are extremely different in appearance.

In the male the top of the head, back, rump and tail are very dark: held in a certain light they appear almost black but they are in reality deep metallic blue or purple. The exact shade of colour varies with the incidence of the light and with the skin we have in our hand at the moment of writing the metallic blue changes to dark metallic green as we change the position of the skin. The wings are blackish-brown with the upper wing-coverts mostly dark chestnut. The throat is pale reddish brown. The remainder of the underparts are yellow.

The hen is almost uniformly dull green in plumage, but the underparts are rather more tinged with yellow than the upper parts. Young males are very much like the females.

During the course of the year the females vary considerably. The feathers become worn and faded and just before the moult there is thus a considerable amount of grey in the plumage.

The adults have the irides reddish brown in colour, the beak dark brown and the legs dirty green with the soles of the toes yellowish.

A male measures about 5 inches in length with a wing of 2½ inches.

Distribution:—This sunbird which is found in Burma and Siam and is common in the Malay Peninsula is also found in Borneo, Sumatra and Java. Further east in the Philippines, Celebes, Flores, etc., the birds are slightly different, the males for instance being much greener on the breast than in local males, but they should no doubt all be included under the specific name of *malaccensis*.

[224]

Drawn by G. A. Levett-Yeats.

THE MALAYAN BROWN-THROATED SUN-BIRD.
Anthreptes malaccensis.

THE BROWN-THROATED SUNBIRD

Status in Singapore:—A very common bird, appearing in the gardens and to be seen in most parts of the island, but it is particularly noticeable that this sunbird seems always to be associated with coconut trees. On the outlying islands it is more numerous than the last-named species which we should say is the predominant sunbird of the public gardens in Singapore.

Field Notes:—Although it may be seen at close quarters in the Botanic Gardens and conveniently examined as it is searching for food flitting about the flowering trees, this bird is most frequently seen in the crowns of the coconut palms.

Other habits:—This sunbird makes a little pear shaped nest which is suspended from a bough. Ridley says that it is composed of bark fibres and the nests of caterpillars and is lined with feathers: also that there is an entrance hole at one side of the nest with a small eave thrown over this hole to protect the interior from rain!

THE LONG-BILLED SPIDER-HUNTER

Arachnothera longirostris longirostris (*Lath.*)

Description:—In the spider-hunters we do not meet with that striking difference between the sexes displayed by the true sunbirds. Males and females are very similar in plumage and differ in detail only. Furthermore the males do not exhibit the bright colours seen in the sunbirds and both sexes partake more or less of that general greenish type of coloration common to the female sunbirds. Both sexes of the present species bear quite a strong resemblance to the female of Maklot's sunbird from which however they can be distinguished by the very long beak.

The colour above is greenish or olive, but the tail is almost black with small whitish tips to the feathers. The throat and upper breast are greyish white and the underparts pale yellow.

The iris is brown, the bill black and slate and the feet slaty or grey in colour.

The total length is about 6 inches but the long curved bill which is one of the characteristic features of the bird may take up 1½ inches of this and so this spider hunter is really about the same in bulk as the brown-throated sunbird.

The wing measures 2½ inches or a little more.

Distribution:—This spider-hunter occurs in India, thence through Burma, Siam, etc., the Malay Peninsula to all the Malaysian islands and Celebes.

Sub-species are recognised from various areas within this range.

Status in Singapore:—Fairly common in Singapore and particularly numerous on Pulau Ubin. Unlike the sunbirds, the spider-hunters do not court publicity by appearing in the bushes, etc., by the side of the garden-paths and other conspicuous places. They like rather the quieter spots and large trees but this and another species are by no means rare in the Botanic Gardens.

Field Notes:—The very long curved bill at once distinguishes the spider-hunters from other local birds. The present species being pale yellow beneath should not be confused with the other kind which occurs (and breeds) in the Botanic Gardens. This second kind has a dark greyish breast and at a short distance looks uniformly dark. It may be known as the grey-breasted spider-hunter (*Arachnothera affinis modesta*). Ridley states that *modesta* haunts the large-leaved gingers and Heliconias in the Gardens.

Other habits:—The food consists to a great extent of insects and spiders for which the bird diligently searches, prying here and there in nooks and crannies, in the creases of the bark of trees and in flowers. The late R. Shelford has published an admirable account of the nest: "The nest is attached to the under surface of a large leaf, and at first sight appears to be composed entirely of skeleton leaves, but a closer examination shows that these are merely the covering of the nest proper, which is a hemispherical cup of inter-woven fibres, apparently the mid-ribs of leaves; it is slung by silken threads to the leaf which supports it, there being a space of less than an inch between the rim of the nest and the under surface of the leaf, just room enough to let the bird creep in. These suspensory threads, which are taken from a spider's web, are passed through holes made in the leaf by the bird's bill and the ends twisted up into knots to prevent slipping. The nest proper is covered over with skeleton leaves the covering extending much beyond the confines of the nest, so that the whole structure appears to be a roughly oval mass. These skeleton leaves are also secured by transverse lashings of spider silk passing through the supporting leaf and knotted at each end. At one end and at the sides of the structure the skeleton leaves are lashed down tightly, but at the other end their attachment is looser, and this marks the entrance to the nest, the mother-bird here creeps under the protective covering of skeleton leaves and so into the nest proper. On the upper surface of the supporting leaf are visible in a double row the knotted ends of the silk threads which sling the nest and serve to keep in position the skeleton leaves. A nest such as this is not only pretty secure from observation but is well protected from snakes, those inveterate destroyers of birds' eggs, moreover, the protective covering of skeleton leaves keeps the nest from swinging about, and there is no danger of the eggs being thrown out, however violently the leaf to which the nest is attached may wave in the breeze.''

FLOWER-PECKERS

Dicœidœ

THE flower-peckers include the smallest of our local birds and all the members of the family are in fact midgets.

They have a much shorter and usually straighter beak than the sunbirds to which they are allied.

In some species the sexes differ in plumage and in these cases the males are extremely handsome birds, often displaying brilliant red or orange in their plumage. In other kinds the sexes are alike and here we find that both are clad in an inconspicuous livery in which dull green plays a prominent part.

Flower-peckers are resident birds with us and probably so everywhere where they are found. Their food consists of insects and seeds.

One observer in Sumatra thinks that the scarlet-backed flower-pecker feeds entirely on the seeds of Loranthus and Viscum.

The nests of these birds are wonderful little structures of exquisite workmanship and in the large majority of cases, in all our common species at least, the eggs are white.

The tops of tall flowering trees are the places where flower-peckers are usually found and this is one reason why the birds are not seen so frequently as their numerical status would appear to justify. Sometimes, by no means rarely in fact, they descend to the lower bushes and on these occasions, if one is quick, these beautiful little birds may be caught with a butterfly net.

Nine species are known from the Malay Peninsula of which the two dealt with below are common in Singapore.

THE ORANGE-BELLIED FLOWER-PECKER

Dicæum trigonostigma trigonostigma (Scop.)

Description:—The male has the top of the head and neck, the wings and tail slaty blue, the chin and throat ashy grey, the breast, abdomen and back bright orange tinged with green on the lower back and rump.

The female lacks all the bright colours of her mate and is mostly olive green, tinged with yellow on the rump and abdomen.

She is usually to be identified in the field by the fact of her very distinctive consort's presence.

The iris is brown, the bill black and the feet slaty or black.

The total length of this tiny bird is about $3\frac{1}{4}$ inches and the wing measures just less than 2 inches.

Distribution:—Burma, Siam, etc., the Malay Peninsula, Borneo, Sumatra and Java, but several sub-species are recognised from within this area.

Status in Singapore:—This is the common flower-pecker of the island and it is by no means a scarce bird although from its habit of frequenting tall trees it escapes popular notice to a great extent.

Field Notes:—Isolated birds or more commonly still small parties, may be seen at times in shrubs in the Botanic Gardens and then on account of the very characteristic colour of the plumage neither this nor the other common local species of flower-pecker can be mistaken. By searching with binoculars the crowns of tall flowering shade trees large numbers of flower-peckers may often be noticed swarming about the topmost branches, very active little birds, and all as busy as bees in a hive: from the top of the tree one hears an almost continually chorus of *chit-chit-chit*.

Drawn by G. A. Levett-Yeats.

THE ORANGE-BELLIED FLOWER-PECKER.
Dicaeum trigonostigma.

THE ORANGE-BELLIED FLOWER-PECKER

Other habits:—Information as to the breeding habits of this bird seems to be very scarce and although it almost certainly breeds in Singapore Island we know of no record of its nest being found on the island.

THE SCARLET-BACKED FLOWER-PECKER

Dicæum cruentatum ignitum (Begbie)

Malay name:—Burong sĕpa putĕri.

Description:—The male has the top of the head and neck and the back bright crimson. The sides of the head and neck are black and the wings glossy black, (a bluish sheen can be seen on the wings when the bird is in the hand). The underparts are creamy white washed with black on the flanks.

The female is quite a different looking bird. She is dull brownish-green above and ashy and buff below. A bright patch of colour is provided by the crimson rump and upper tail-coverts.

The iris is dark brown, the bill and feet black.

Total length about 3½ inches; wing nearly 2 inches.

Distribution:—Ignoring small differences in plumage it may be said that this flower-pecker is found in India, Burma, Southern China, Siam, the Malay Peninsula, Borneo, Sumatra and Java.

Local status:—Not so common as the orange-bellied flower-pecker but far from rare and frequenting much the same kind of situations as that bird. On the outlying islands the circumstances are reversed and *ignitum* seems to be the commoner species of the two.

Field Notes:—We have little to add to the remarks placed under this heading in the last species dealt with as they apply equally well to the present bird.

Other habits:—In the absence of first-hand observation on the matter of the nidification of this flower-pecker we have been tempted to quote the following account written by an ornithologist who worked in India:—

"The nest is generally built in mango-trees but other trees, especially if the leaves are large and drooping, are also used. It is placed at all heights from the ground, from twelve feet to the summits of the highest trees. The nest is suspended from an outside twig, and is so surrounded by leaves that it is almost invisible. When once the female begins to set, all efforts to find the nest would, I believe, be useless. It is only by watching the little birds carrying materials, which they do incessantly and with a constant twitter, that I and my shikaree have been able to secure the nests.

"To say that the nest is most beautiful is only to say what is applicable to the nest of all the flower-peckers. The nest of this little bird is simply exquisite when newly built. It measures no more than 4 inches in total height, and one nest I have is only $3\frac{1}{2}$ inches. It is egg-shaped, slightly pointed at the upper end, where it is attached to the branch. Its external diameter is 2 inches. The entrance is circular $\frac{3}{4}$ inch diameter, and placed just mid-way between the top and bottom of the nest. The egg-chamber is small, the walls of the nest being of considerable thickness."

"The bulk of the nest is made of finest vegetable down of dazzling whiteness resembling spun glass, and exteriorly the nest is kept firm by being bound round with fine grass, which is twisted into a rope at the lower edge of the entrance. At the back of one nest there are a few patches of excreta of caterpillars, and in another, four dry blossoms of some shrub are stuck to the back of the nest. As a rule, however, no ornamentation is attempted."

We can very appropriately wind up the account of the last bird we are to describe in detail in this volume with the above description. It is from the pen of E. W. Oates whose name with that of A. O. Hume will always be associated with the study of ornithology in the East. The paragraph which we quote furthermore provides a most excellent example of the manner in which such observations should be framed.

OTHER PERCHING BIRDS

THE only wren known from the Malay Peninsula is a small and rare bird (*Pnœpyga*) found in the mountains.

The titmice are likewise very scarce as regards species in this part of the world and are more numerous in the northern parts of the Old World. The two Malayan species are only entitled to passing notice here although one, a striking black and yellow species (*Melanochlora*) was recorded from Singapore many years ago.

The nuthatches, crows and buntings all well-known birds to the European must also be dismissed in a few words. The two species of nuthatch found on the mainland do not occur in Singapore.

The crows are represented in Singapore by the casual appearance of the jungle crow (*Corvus coronoides macrorhynchus*). The occurences must be very casual indeed as we have not seen a crow in five years residence on the island. Many years ago there appears to have been an attempt to introduce the house crow of India into Singapore but the effort did not meet with success a fact probably not to be deplored!

The single bunting known from Malaya is *Emberiza aureola* and this is only a winter visitor.

The white-eyes (Fam. *Zosteropidæ*) are tiny birds of greenish-yellow plumage. They owe their English name to the presence of a circle of white feathers round the eye. Hume's white-eye is recorded from Singapore: numbers of live white-eyes are brought into Singapore by Chinese traders and sold as cage-birds.

An oriole occurs not rarely in Singapore. This is the black-naped oriole (*Oriolus chinensis indicus*). The adult male is entirely bright yellow with black markings but the female has the back tinged with green. In young birds there are thin

black streaks on the breast. The length is about 11 inches.
This oriole spends the summer in China, Mongolia, etc.
coming south in the winter but a few birds certainly stay over
the summer in Singapore although perhaps they do not breed.
One or two orioles kept in the vicinity of Sepoy Lines for the
whole of 1925 and could be seen or heard in every month.
Another local bird very familiar in appearance to Europeans
on account of its strong resemblance to the "titlark" is the
Malayan pipit (*Anthus richardi malayensis*). This is indeed so
like the meadow pipit of Great Britain that it requires no
further description. It is fairly common in Singapore. Certain other "passeres" may be noticed in Singapore but we can,
on account of our limited space, do little more than mention
them here.

Several "yellow" wagtails occur as migrants (no "pied"
species is known locally). The commonest of these is *Motacilla
flava simillima* but another bird with a much longer tail is also
met with. This latter is the eastern representative of the well-
known grey-wagtail of Britain. Yet another wagtail, but this
time a tree haunting bird rather than a ground lover occurs as
a visitor. This is the forest-wagtail (*Dendronathus indicus*).
Seen in the trees its characteristic features are the very pale
breast with conspicuous black markings on the throat.

The only bullfinch known from Malaya is restricted to the
mountains of the mainland.

Certain starlings with white in their plumage may be seen
in Singapore. These belong to the genus *Sturnia* and it would
appear that their ranks are swollen by the addition of escaped
cage-birds for they are very popular as pets.

With the exception of the tailor-birds already mentioned
very few warblers are known from the island. In grass-lands
a tiny heavily streaked species of *Cisticola* may sometimes
be seen but it is not very common. More numerous in
such localities is a wren-warbler, *Burnesia flaviventris* which
is *not* streaked, has a longish tail and yellowish underparts. A
bird very like the willow-warbler and chiffchaff of the British
Isles may be seen in the winter. This may be known as the
Arctic willow-warbler, *Phylloscopus borealis*.

[235]

INDEX TO POPULAR NAMES *

*Only the main reference is given.

[238]

PAGE | | PAGE

[239]

[241]

INDEX TO TECHNICAL NAMES *

*Only the main reference is given.

PAGE

INDEX TO MALAY NAMES